COLD WAR
SCOTLAND

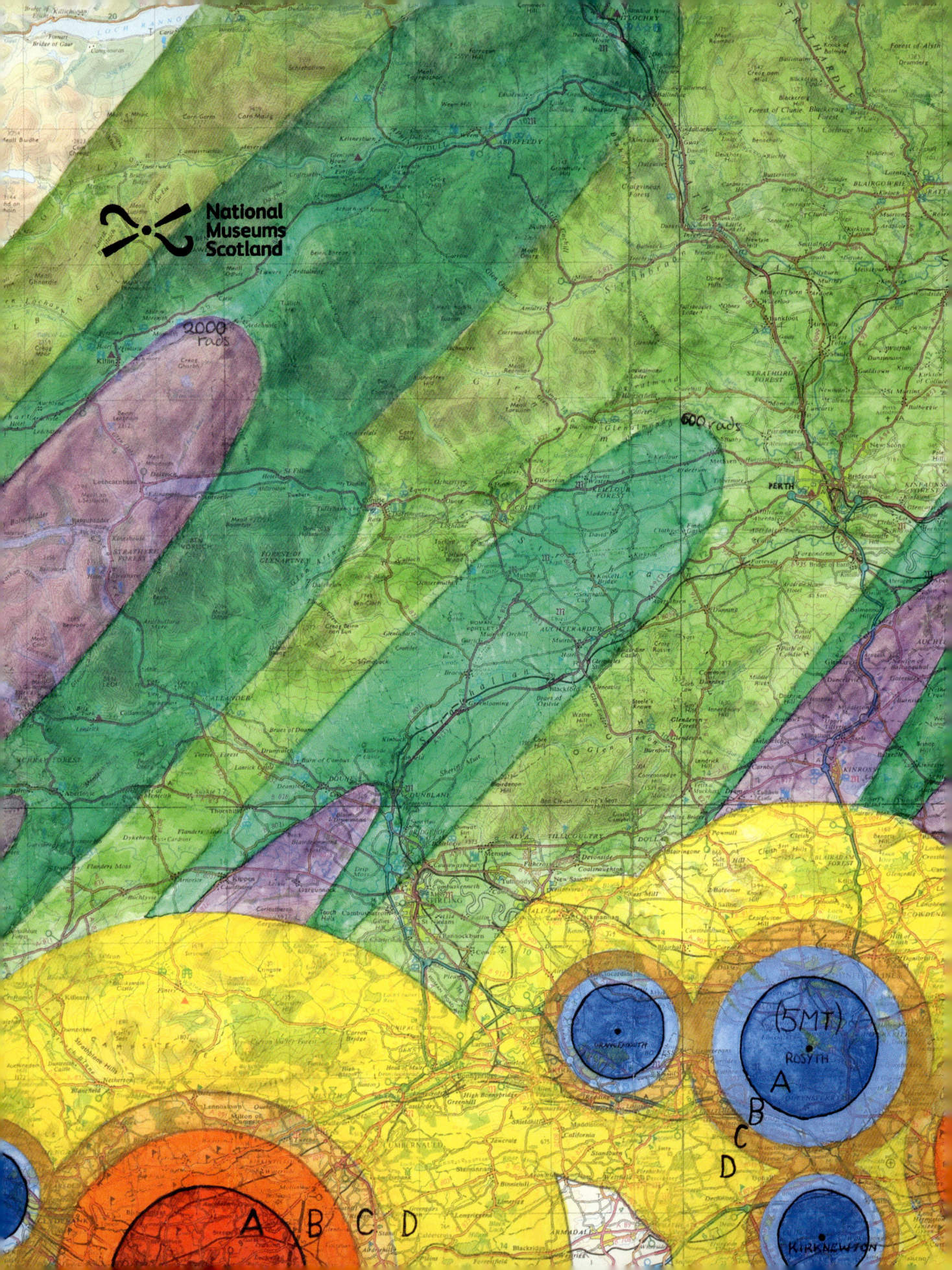

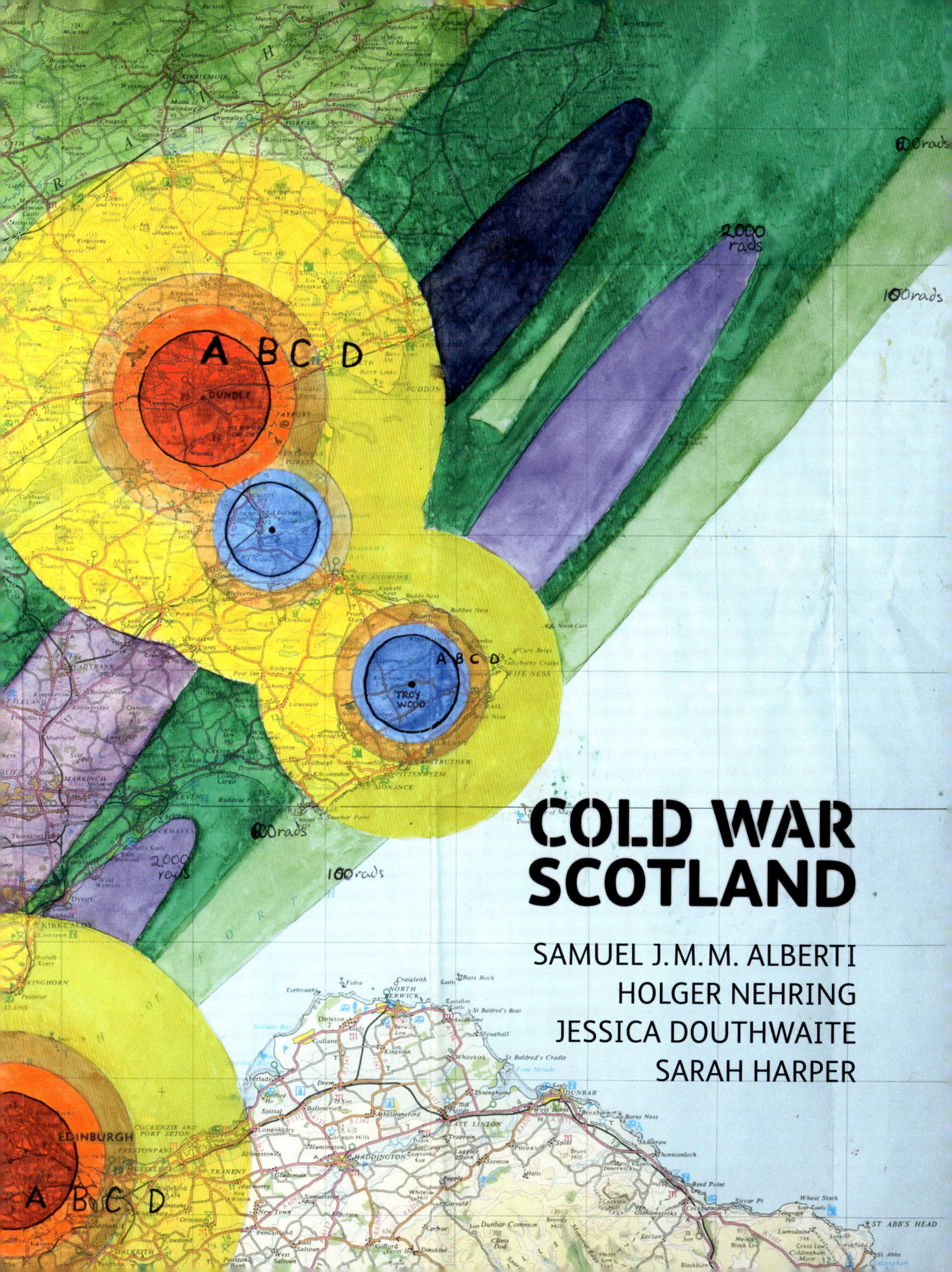

COLD WAR SCOTLAND

SAMUEL J. M. M. ALBERTI
HOLGER NEHRING
JESSICA DOUTHWAITE
SARAH HARPER

Cold War Scotland

An exhibition at
National Museum of Scotland
Chambers Street
Edinburgh EH1 1JF

www.nms.ac.uk

13 July 2024 – 26 January 2025

Book published in 2024 by
NMS Enterprises Limited – Publishing
a division of NMS Enterprises Limited
National Museums Scotland
Chambers Street
Edinburgh EH1 1JF

www.nms.ac.uk

Text, photographs and illustrations
© National Museums Scotland 2024
(unless otherwise credited)

No part of this publication may be reproduced, stored in a retrieval system, or transmitted in any form or by any means, electronic, mechanical, photocopying, recording or otherwise, without the prior written permission of the publisher.

The rights of the contributors and artists to be identified as the authors and illustrators of this book have been asserted by them in accordance with the Copyright, Designs and Patents Act 1988.

British Library Cataloguing in Publication Data
A catalogue record of this book is available from the British Library.

ISBN 978 1 910682 52 4

Book design and typesetting by NMS Enterprises Limited – Publishing.
Cover design by Mark Blackadder.
Printed and bound in Great Britain by Bell & Bain Limited, Glasgow.

This product is made of material from well-managed, FSC®-certified forests and other controlled sources.

For a full listing of NMS Enterprises Limited – Publishing titles and related merchandise:

www.nms.ac.uk/books

Contents

Foreword by Chris Breward 6

Acknowledgements 8

Image and text credits 9

Introduction: Hopes and fears 12

Chapter 1: Nuclear nation 26

Chapter 2: Mobilising Scotland 54

Chapter 3: Cold War connections 82

Chapter 4: Material memories 108

Epilogue: Sensing the Cold War 124

Further reading 127

Foreword

Chris Breward
DIRECTOR, NATIONAL MUSEUMS SCOTLAND

For nearly five decades the Cold War shaped Scottish life and landscape, and its legacies endure today. This book, like the exhibition it accompanies at the National Museum of Scotland (July 2024 to January 2025), explores the impact on Scotland's social, political and technical history.

Cold War Scotland arose from a research project generously funded by the UK Arts and Humanities Research Council, 'Materialising the Cold War'. My colleagues in National Museums Scotland worked alongside researchers and curators at the University of Stirling, Imperial War Museums, Royal Airforce Museums, and collaborators further afield including the Norsk Luftfartsmuseum, Bodø, Norway, and the Allied Museum in Berlin. They asked how the superpower conflict is represented by museums with material culture and how people respond to these objects.

During the course of their research the team studied not only nuclear bombs, but also peace badges and international artwork. They found evidence of hope as well as fear, of suspicion but also friendship, across the Iron Curtain. Many of these objects and the stories they tell are shown for the first time in *Cold War Scotland*. They are more important than ever given the context of the ongoing war in Ukraine: for although this book is about twentieth-century Scotland and the Cold War, it helps us to put into historical context the active conflict in the former Soviet Union.

We believe that the research project 'Materialising the Cold War' does exactly what museum initiatives should do: it shows how relevant museum collections are in addressing the challenges of our age. *Cold War Scotland* deepens knowledge of the artefacts in our care and enhances their meanings for existing and new audiences.

June 2024

Nuclear weapon effects computer

This slide rule could have been used to measure the potential damage and devastation caused by a nuclear attack. Scales and measurements are given to estimate the power of the bomb, size of the resultant crater and even the percentage of people trapped or killed.

Image © National Museums Scotland

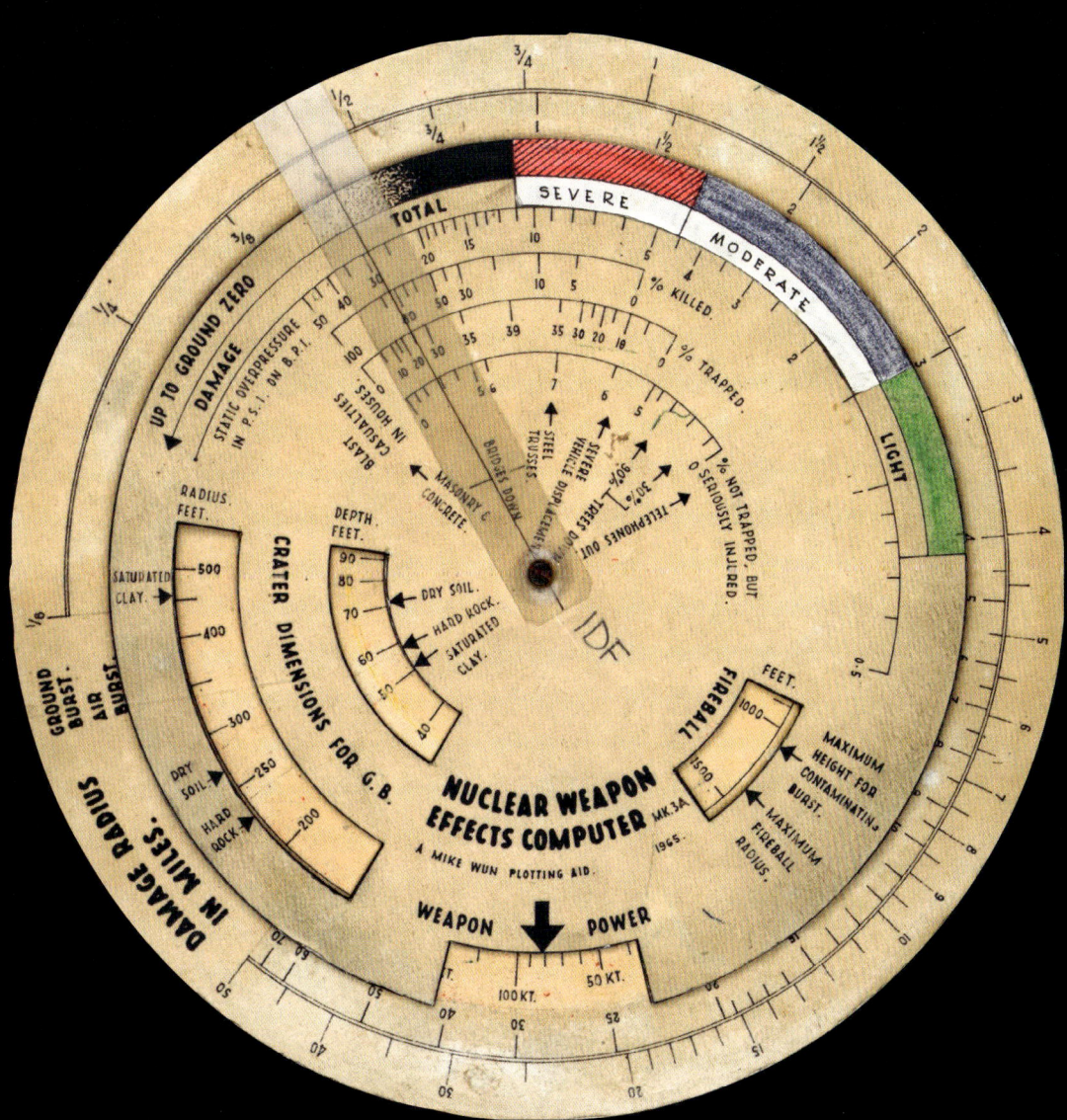

Acknowledgements

All books are the result of teamwork, but *Cold War Scotland* especially so.

The four co-authors were inspired at the outset by Trevor Royle's pathbreaking *Facing the Bear: Scotland and the Cold War* and Sarah Harper's doctoral work 'Bombers, Bunkers, and Badges: The Cold War Materialised in National Museums Scotland'.

We were greatly aided by Meredith Greiling and Jim Gledhill as we wrote the book alongside the accompanying exhibition. Ian Brown has been helpful throughout, as have other curatorial colleagues. Photographers and members of the Collections Services department at National Museums Scotland generated the stunning images of museum objects, and we are grateful to the individuals and organisations who supplied and granted permission for the additional images.

Stuart Allan and Sarah Laurenson read the entire work and provided insightful comments. John Livingston, club historian at Kilmarnock Football Club, assisted with research and access. We would also like to thank our colleagues in the publishing arm of National Museums Scotland Enterprises; and we are grateful for the patience of Linden Williamson. All errors are our own of course.

Cold War Scotland stemmed from 'Materialising the Cold War', a research project funded by the UK Arts and Humanities Research Council (Project Reference AH/V001078/1), based at National Museums Scotland and the University of Stirling.

Samuel J. M. M. Alberti
Holger Nehring
Jessica Douthwaite
Sarah Harper

Image and text credits

No reproduction of material in copyright is permitted without prior contact with the publisher. Every attempt has been made to contact copyright holders to use the material in this publication. If any image or quote has been inadvertently missed, please contact the publisher. Acknowledgements for use of source material and photographs within this publication are as follows:

IMAGES / PHOTOGRAPHS

Alamy and their image contributors
Annandale Observer / Heritage Service, Dumfries & Galloway Council
Barnton Bunker
Dandare Corporation Ltd
Glasgow City Archives
Paul Grimes
Sarah Harper
Historic Environment Scotland
 – Canmore
 – Sir Basil Spence Archive
Imperial War Museums
Peter Kennard
National Archives
National Galleries of Scotland
National Library of Scotland
National Museums Scotland
Nuclear Decommissioning Authority
Nuclear Restoration Services
Michael Sanders
SCRAN (Historic Environment Scotland)
 – *Herald & Evening Times* (Newsquest)
 – The Scotsman Publications
 – West of Scotland Archaeology Service
SWNS Media Group
Ullapool Museum Trust
University of Dundee, The Peto Collection

TEXT

Argyll Publishing for extracts from Andrene Messersmith, *The American Years: Dunoon & the US Navy*, 2003, 2023, available from thirstybooks.com
Cambridge University Press for the extract from David Edgerton, *Warfare State: Britain, 1920–1970*, 2006
Carcanet Press for the extract from Hugh MacDiarmid, 'Third Hymn to Lenin the Soviet Revolutionary', 1957
Devil's Porridge Museum
Dounreay Oral History Project
Edinburgh University Press Ltd for extracts from Angela Bartie, *The Edinburgh Festivals*, 2013
Kilmarnock Football Club
Liverpool University Press for the extract from Wayne D. Cocroft, Roger J. C. Thomas and P. S. Barnwell (ed.), *Cold War: Building for Nuclear Confrontation, 1946–1989*, 2004
Pluto Books Ltd for extracts from Malcolm Spaven, *Fortress Scotland: A Guide to the Military Presence*, 1983
Studies in Photography, https://studiesinphotography.com/
University of Edinburgh Scotland-Russia: Cultural Encounters Since 1900 Project

Introduction

Hopes and fears

In the autumn of 1962, the world was on the brink of nuclear war, and Scotland was a potential battlefield. American bombers stationed on British air bases were loaded with nuclear weapons, with crews in a state of constant readiness. Vulcan bombers of the Royal Air Force were on what was known as 'Quick Reaction Alert' – able to take off within 15 minutes. The 59 Thor nuclear missiles positioned across Britain were also on standby; and six submarines stationed at the Holy Loch – half an hour's drive from Glasgow – were at sea, fully armed with nuclear missiles. Only 17 years after the end of the Second World War, Scots, like many others in the United Kingdom and around the world, once again feared that war was coming.[1]

The immediate cause for the alert was a dispute between the United States (of America/US) and the Union of Soviet Socialist Republics (Soviet Union/USSR) over the stationing of Soviet nuclear missiles on Cuba. These missiles could have reached the continental United States, less than 100 miles away. The Soviet action had been prompted by the American deployment of nuclear-capable missiles to Turkey – too close for comfort for the Soviet Union. In the end, diplomacy averted disaster, but for 13 days the threat of nuclear annihilation loomed large. This episode became known as the Cuban Missile Crisis.

A global confrontation

The controversy over the Cuban missiles followed clashes between the United States, the Soviet Union and their respective allies from the late 1950s into the early '60s. These were mainly about the status of Germany – at that time divided into a liberal-democratic West and a socialist East – and what this meant for the relationship between the different parties. One of those crises was the construction of a fence between East and West Berlin in August 1961 – the origins of the Berlin Wall and the fortified border between the western Federal Republic of Germany and the eastern German Democratic Republic.

Pages 10–11: Aerial view of the Holy Loch while in use by the US Navy

From 1961, the picturesque Holy Loch, on the coast of the Firth of Clyde, became the home of some of the US Navy's most powerful nuclear submarines. Thousands of American personnel and their families embedded themselves into local communities, particularly Dunoon, until the closure of the base in 1992.

© West of Scotland Archaeology Service. Licensor www.SCRAN.ac.uk

Berlin Wall

Berlin became the epicentre of Cold War tensions as the city was divided into a liberal-democratic West and a socialist East. In 1961, the Soviet-controlled German Democratic Republic erected a 155-km wall to prevent people escaping to the West.

United Archives GmbH / Alamy Stock Photo

The underlying conflict was the ideological and military confrontation between the United States and the Soviet Union known as the Cold War. The term 'Cold War' had been used in 1930s Britain to describe the foreign policies of National Socialist (Nazi) Germany towards its Eastern neighbours, but the British writer George Orwell is said to have been the first to apply it to the context we use today. In an essay on the consequences of nuclear weapons for international politics published in October 1945, he envisioned that 'two or three monstrous super-states' would emerge, 'each possessed of a weapon by which millions of people can be wiped out in a few seconds, dividing the world between them'. He predicted that this scenario would 'put an end to large-scale wars at the cost of prolonging indefinitely a "peace that is no peace"'.[2]

The term was subsequently made popular by the American journalist Walter Lippman, who wrote essays arguing against the emergence of such a Cold War. He advocated preserving what was left of the wartime alliance between the United States, United Kingdom and Soviet Union to prevent a global catastrophe.

Lippman argued in vain. The rivalry between the United States and the Soviet Union emerged from the rubble of the Second World War and focused on particular areas in Europe and Asia, especially Germany, Korea and Vietnam. Who would control these countries, and how? These questions had an impact on politics and society around the world. The United States and its Western allies worked together in the alliance of the North Atlantic Treaty Organization (NATO), founded in 1949; six years later the Soviet Union integrated its allies in the Warsaw Pact.

From an ideological perspective, this Cold War was a clash of two empires: the American empire based on liberal democracy and capitalism that in principle worked through consent; and the Soviet empire which emphasised socialist planning, centralised control and took the form of dictatorships.[3] But in contrast to what the term 'Cold War' suggests, this was anything but a frozen conflict. While the lines of control were drawn on the world map by the early 1960s, politics, society and culture around the world continued to be influenced by the Cold War.

Depending on their political and socio-economic interests, countries outside Europe positioned themselves in different ways to this Cold War confrontation. Former colonies used their relationship with the superpowers (the United States and the Soviet Union) to pursue national independence, often with bloody consequences. The Cold War outside Europe was therefore anything but cold – one historian has called the non-European world 'the Cold War's killing fields'.[4]

Around the world, however, the Cold War was not just about fears of a confrontation involving nuclear weapons, or an attack by the other side on one's own territories; it was also about the hopes of creating a better world after the destruction and violence of the Second World War. Cold War history is about how these hopes and fears were intertwined.

Scottish experiences

Scotland was constitutionally part of the United Kingdom during the Cold War, and the armed forces and other institutions were centrally controlled. Nevertheless Scotland's people and, in particular, the country's landscape played a distinct role in this global superpower confrontation. For such a small country, it was connected to the Cold War in many ways and its population played an active role in shaping it.

Geographically, Scotland was in an ideal position for the Western alliance. With its long coastline, it guarded the entry point to the passage that ran from the Soviet Union via Norway, Iceland and Greenland to North America – the so-called 'GIUK Gap' (Greenland, Iceland and the United Kingdom). The control of this passage would be of crucial importance for fending off a potential Soviet offensive.

Scotland also had airfields and ports that had been expanded during the Second World War from 1939–45. Its relative proximity to the Soviet Union meant that it was an ideal position for building intelligence installations. Its mountains and islands offered ideal areas for rugged-terrain training or weapons testing. With the concentration of heavy industry in the central area between Glasgow in the west and Edinburgh in the east, it could also provide essential defence infrastructure production.

During the Cold War, the Scottish coastline and its islands became integral parts of Britain's warfare state, with the east coast well suited to intelligence installations. RAF Edzell in Angus was a key component of the British and American intelligence operation and the sizeable air force bases at Kinloss and Lossiemouth played important roles in

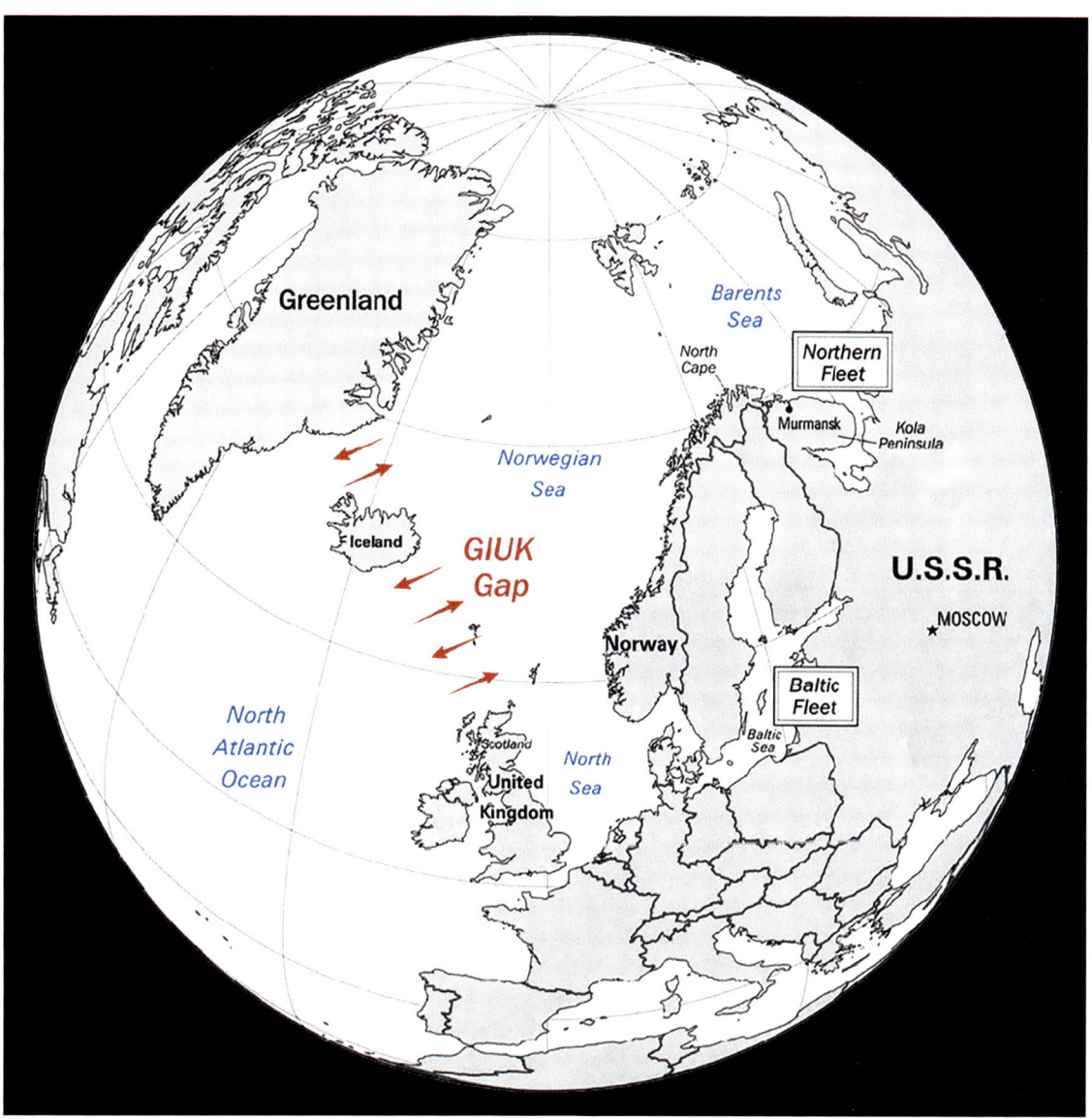

Map of Greenland, Iceland, United Kingdon Gap

Scotland became a Cold War frontline due to the geographical positioning in the GIUK Gap made up of Greenland, Iceland and the United Kingdom. This gap was the naval choke point and passageway in the northern Atlantic Ocean between the United States and the Soviet Union.

Public domain, via Wikimedia Commons

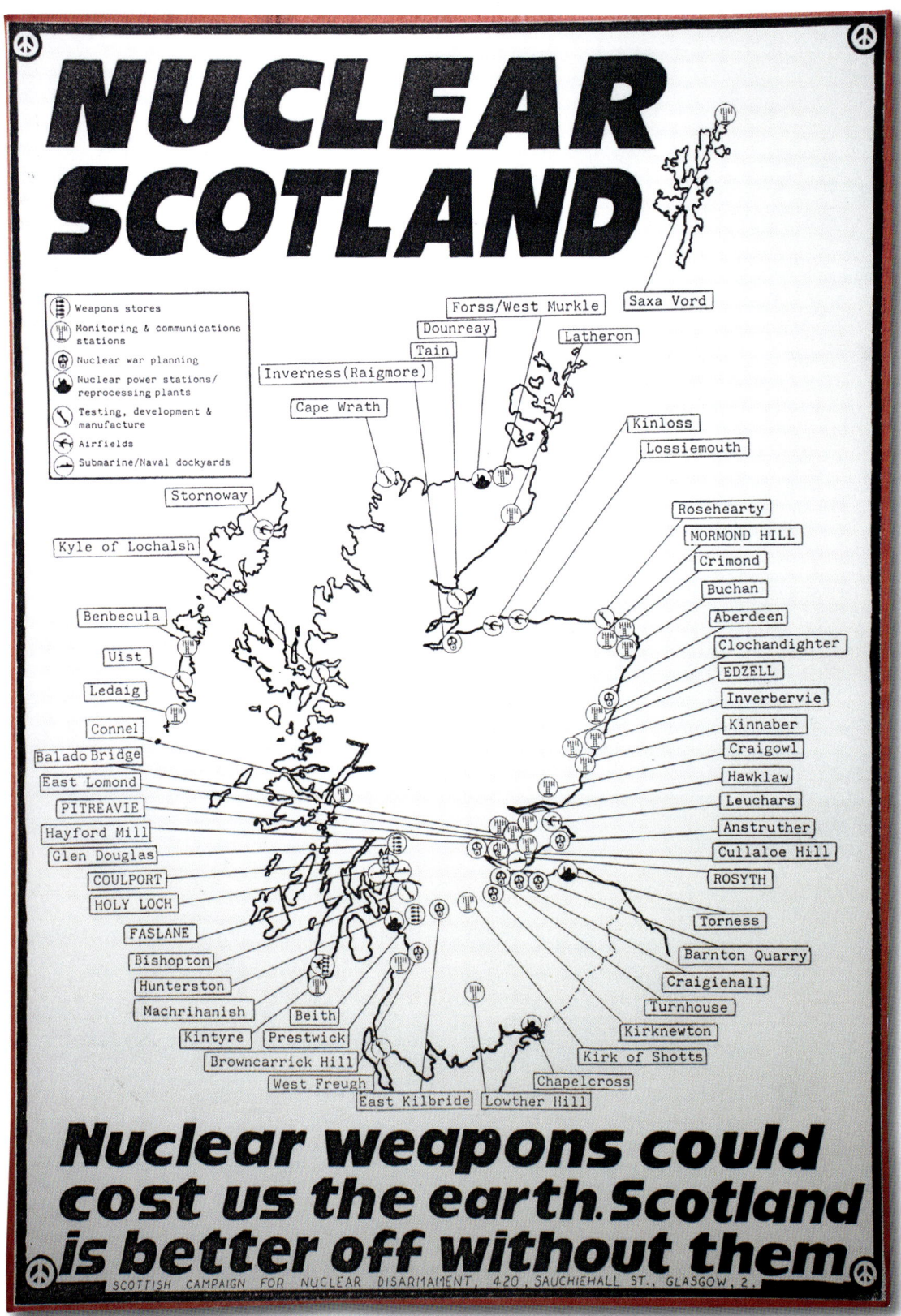

RAF Edzell

In 1960, the US Air Force used the geographical position of the former RAF Edzell base to establish the Naval Security Group Oceanographic Monitoring Station. Intelligence, military and civilian staff monitored Soviet Navy and submarine activities from Edzell using code breaking and satellite technologies.

NB/ROD / Alamy Stock Photo

Opposite: Nuclear Scotland map, c.1980s

The Scottish Campaign for Nuclear Disarmament produced this annotated map to highlight military and nuclear sites across Scotland. Capitalised names indicated potential Soviet targets, such as Rosyth, Faslane and Edzell.

Image © National Museums Scotland

the sea defences of the United Kingdom and NATO, sending out aircraft to patrol for ships and submarines. Mormond Hill in Aberdeenshire, for example, was the centre for military communications in Scotland and beyond. It hosted military radio facilities that linked European countries with North America and would have played a major role in a nuclear war. Cape Wrath, on the rugged north coast, offered a unique area for the Royal Navy and allied forces to train for sea warfare. On the northern tip of the north isles, the radar facility at Saxa Vord on Unst, Shetland, was a key component for detecting Soviet attacks on the United Kingdom and its allies – and is operational again today.

From the 1960s, submarine bases on the west coast housed the nuclear weapons intended to deter an attack on Britain. The Holy Loch, on the Cowal peninsula, Firth of Clyde, was home to the US Navy's largest overseas nuclear submarine base (see pages 34–37), while the United Kingdom's nuclear deterrent was based at nearby Faslane on the Gare Loch.

Scotland's Central Belt offered a home to important logistical and industrial sites, such as the Rosyth Dockyard on the River Forth, where nuclear submarines and the surface fleet were maintained. Across the Forth was the refinery at Grangemouth, also used for military purposes, as well as a number of command and control facilities such as the Barnton Quarry bunker in Edinburgh.

In the south-west of Scotland, the nuclear reactor at Chapelcross in Annan, Dumfriesshire, completed in 1959, was built not only to generate electricity but also to produce fuel for the United Kingdom's nuclear weapons.

In exploring such sites, this book – alongside the 2024 exhibition at the National Museum of Scotland – will examine the Scottish experience of the global Cold War at the frontline. With our focus less on the diplomatic history of the superpower conflict, we will look instead at what happened in Scotland, and the impact on the people there and on Scots elsewhere. To do so, we will take the reader on a journey back to the Cold War by considering three important points.

In Chapter 1, we will examine the nuclear arms race. This was central to the Cold War and involved the acquisition of ever more deadly nuclear weapons by the United States, the Soviet Union, and some of their allies. Ironically, it was probably this ability of both sides to obliterate each other that explains why the Cold War did not result in the outbreak of violent hostilities in Europe and the North Atlantic. No politician wanted to take the risk of destroying their own country by launching a nuclear attack on another.

Consequently, Chapter 1 will also investigate the impact of nuclear weapons and the development of nuclear power on Scottish society. It will show how military and civilian nuclear technology were closely linked, sparking both fears of nuclear war and hopes for economic and social regeneration through plentiful electricity, and ask how these twin developments impacted upon Scottish life.

In Chapter 2, we will look at mobilisation. Wars are about mobilisation: the mobilisation of people for the purposes of war, the mobilisation of the economy to support the war, and the mobilisation of society to create legitimacy for war. We will ask how anti-communism percolated all areas of society, including religion, and show how Scots participated in the Cold War: by doing national service, serving in the Royal Observer Corps for civil defence, and working in defence-related industries.

This chapter will further consider how people mobilised *against* war, with the rise of a powerful movement protesting against nuclear weapons and various local campaigns concerning military installations. By regarding the Cold War as a real war, peace movement activists campaigned for a different society. In doing so, they also created an image of Scotland as a threatened nation and as a community of hope against destruction.

In Chapter 3, we will address how these mobilisations were connected to the world beyond Scotland and consider how Scottish communities interacted with American service personnel and their families. We will also discuss the many connections formed with Eastern European countries and the Soviet Union during the Cold War through, for example, interactions with Soviet trawlermen in Ullapool, political initiatives such as the Edinburgh Conversations in the 1980s, or tourism behind the so-called 'Iron Curtain'.

Royal Observer Corps crest

The crest of the Royal Observer Corps depicts an Elizabethan Beacon Lighter who forewarned the arrival of the Spanish Armada (1588). This also inspired the ROC motto 'Forewarned is Forearmed'.

Image © National Museums Scotland

The Iron Curtain and other Cold War objects

The Cold War ended with the collapse of the Iron Curtain around 1989. The term 'iron curtain' originally referred to the protective sheet lowered onto the stage in a theatre in case of fire. Its use to indicate the division of the world between the capitalist 'West' and the 'East' under Soviet control goes back to a speech by Winston Churchill.

Churchill had been the Conservative British Prime Minister during the Second World War but in July 1945 lost the General Election to Clement Attlee's Labour Party. The former Prime Minister first used the term in his speech on the 'Sinews of Peace' at a college in the United States in March 1946:

> From Stettin in the Baltic to Trieste in the Adriatic, an iron curtain has descended across the Continent. Behind that line lie all the capitals of the ancient states of Central and Eastern Europe. Warsaw, Berlin, Prague, Vienna, Budapest, Belgrade, Bucharest and Sofia, all these famous cities and the populations around them lie in what I must call the Soviet sphere, and all are subject in one form or another, not only to Soviet influence but to a very high and, in many cases, increasing measure of control from Moscow.[5]

Here, Churchill argued for a prudent policy towards the Soviet Union and a special alliance between the United States and United Kingdom, but it came

Winston Churchill's 'Iron Curtain' speech

British wartime Prime Minister Winston Churchill's speech in Fulton, Missouri popularised the term 'Iron Curtain'. He was referring to the division of Europe after the Second World War and the Soviet influence over Eastern Europe.

Fremantle / Alamy Stock Photo

Fall of the Berlin Wall

On the evening of 9 November 1989 the Berlin Wall fell, allowing Berliners to move between East and West. For many, the fall of the Wall marked the end of the Cold War in Europe.

imageBROKER.com GmbH & Co. KG / Alamy Stock Photo

at a time when the latter relationship was anything but smooth. There were questions about how the financially challenged United Kingdom would repay the United States for its military and economic assistance during the Second World War. There were also questions about whether the Americans, keen to maintain their nuclear monopoly, would share information on developing nuclear weapons with the British (whose scientists had played a major role in developing these weapons in the first place). The deployment of the US military in Scotland which we explore in the following chapters was one way that the relationship between the United States and the United Kingdom would be strengthened after this period of uncertainty.

The Iron Curtain, as manifested in the Berlin Wall, was really made out of concrete, barbed wire and mesh, guarded by lines of border posts and watchtowers. But it came to stand as the real and symbolic boundary between the American and Soviet spheres of influence in Europe. The Berlin Wall's downfall – and the subsequent collapse of the Soviet Union in 1991 – signalled the end of the Cold War.

For Scotland, the fall of the Iron Curtain coincided with a reduced presence of armed forces, although there are still a number of military installations in the country, including the Royal Navy's submarine base in Faslane. Airfields and bunkers have been converted into museums and many of the buildings that formed part of the critical military infrastructure are now falling apart. The Cold War is no longer a lived experience. As discussed in Chapter 4, it has become part of Scottish history, memory and heritage.

Materialising the Cold War

The story of the Cold War has often been told as one centred on words: the words of diplomats and military officers in orders and memoranda; of politicians in speeches; of peace protesters on demonstrations. Words are the fundamental way we can grasp our history. But words often emerge by engaging with material objects: by describing them, using them, or reflecting on our experiences with them.

As well as considering arguments and texts, this book also considers the ways objects can speak to us – and how people in the past and the present have made sense of them. There have been books about the material objects linked to the Cold War before, but these have usually focused on one particular area, such as art and design.[6] This time, we want to highlight how Scottish experiences of the Cold War more generally can be told by considering objects alongside images and texts.

By looking at Cold War experiences not only through individual people but also through the stories of objects, *Cold War Scotland* highlights how fears and hopes, violence and reconstruction, transformation and conservatism were intimately linked to each other. Many contemporaries remember the period as a time of happiness and affluence rather than war and violence. Thankfully, nuclear war remained imaginary in Europe and North America, played out in war games and in apocalyptic imaginations. But if we know where to look, preparations for this global war, and other experiences of fear and hope, had concrete material manifestations. It is these objects and the experiences they speak of that form the basis of this book.

We begin with the story of the first transatlantic telephone cable ('TAT-1'), which tells us how the Cold War came to be connected to Scotland, and how Scots connected themselves to the Cold War.

Notes

1. Trevor Royle, *Facing the Bear: Scotland and the Cold War* (Edinburgh: Birlinn, 2019).
2. George Orwell, 'You and the Atom Bomb', *Tribune*, 19 October 1945, available at https://gutenberg.net.au/ebooks03/0300011h.html#part33, following Matthew Grant and Benjamin Ziemann, 'Introduction: the Cold War as an imaginary war', in idem, eds., *Understanding the Imaginary War. Culture, Thought and Nuclear Conflict, 1945–1990* (Manchester: Manchester University Press, 2016), p. 1.
3. Odd Arne Westad, *Global Cold War: Third World Interventions and the Making of Our Times* (Cambridge: Cambridge University Press, 2007).
4. Paul Chamberlin, *The Cold War's Killing Fields* (New York: Harper, 2018).
5. Winston Churchill, 'The Sinews of Peace', 5 March 1946, https://winstonchurchill.org/resources/speeches/1946-1963-elder-statesman/the-sinews-of-peace.
6. For example, David Crowley and Jane Pavitt (eds), *Cold War Modern: Design 1945–1970* (London: V&A, 2008).

TAT-1: Transatlantic Telephone Cable 1

The British Postmaster General announced the decision to lay a transatlantic telephone cable on 1 December 1953. The purpose of the cable, known as TAT-1 (Transatlantic Telephone Cable 1), was to make communications across the Atlantic better and allow for the expansion of telecommunications.

The project was a collaboration between the British General Post Office (GPO), the Canadian Overseas Telecommunications Operation and the American Telephone and Telegraph Company, which were then not private companies but extensions of the state.

TAT-1 consisted of two cables laid between Oban in Argyll and Bute, Scotland, and Clarenville in Newfoundland, Canada, to facilitate communications between the United States and the Soviet Union. Today, the entry point of the cable is a rather mundane concrete shaft in a scenic location at a small bay on the Gallanach Estate a few miles south of Oban on the west coast. The modernist building that was home to the technical installation is now derelict. There is little to suggest that this site has any major historical relevance.

At the opening ceremony in Oban on 25 September 1956, the focus was not on superpower competition, but rather on national ingenuity. Speaker after speaker stressed British engineering prowess and the bravery of British sailors aboard HMTS *Monarch*, one of the GPO's cable-laying ships, that had made the venture possible.

Nonetheless, the cable had direct Cold War connections. Notably, speakers at the Canadian and American opening ceremonies on the other side of the Atlantic were more explicit than their British counterparts when pointing out that the cable enabled much better and faster communications between the United States and its allies in Europe, especially the United Kingdom. This, they argued, would be a major advantage in a war against the Soviet Union.

From the 1930s, the British military had taken a keen interest in laying a transatlantic telephone cable to improve the imperial communications network. In the early 1950s, classified communications within the British military highlighted potential military uses of the new cable. From 1963, TAT-1 carried the direct line between the White House in Washington through Oban, via London and Scandinavia, to the Kremlin in Moscow.

Although we often imagine this 'hotline' to have linked two red telephones, it was, in reality, a line connecting two telex machines – automatic typewriters that converted sound into letters. For the most part, they transmitted nonsensical messages to test the line. When new forms of communication were later introduced, TAT-1 continued to operate as a reserve. Although the hotline is often interpreted as a symbol of peace and negotiation, we now know that the US military regarded it as an important channel through which it could communicate warnings and threats to the Soviet Union during a nuclear war.

The location of the entry point near the small town of Oban highlights that the Cold War in Scotland was not just a matter for Scots living in cities; it also had a direct impact on small towns and the surrounding countryside. On the back of the installation of a new transatlantic line, the telephone trunk lines towards Inverness and Glasgow, and from there towards England, were modernised. The larger capacity enabled the expansion of telephone systems into the Scottish Highlands as well as its electrification, just as the installation of radar stations had often driven the electrification of remoter areas in the islands.

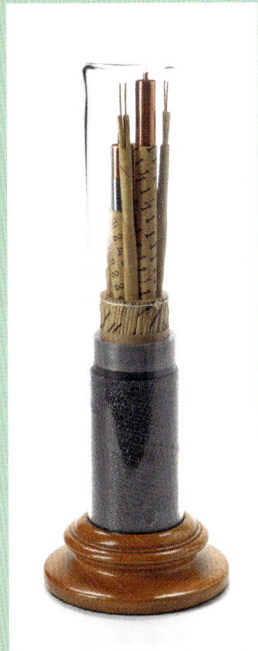

While Cold War developments were not the only driver of the expansion of telephone services and the electrification of more rural areas, it is difficult to imagine that these changes would have happened as swiftly. These networks and other elements of Cold War infrastructure, also including roads leading to bases and military installations, became parts of the Scottish rural landscape that are now rarely noticed. We will return to reflect on these remnants in Chapter 4.

The cable could also be used to subvert governmental authority during the Cold War. On 26 May 1957 the activist Paul Robeson, whom we will encounter in Chapter 3, broadcast a concert from New York to St Pancras Town Hall in London. The cable helped Robeson to circumvent the travel restrictions that the US Government had imposed on him because of his sympathies for communism.

Presentation samples of the cable, prepared for the grand opening, survive in the collection of National Museums Scotland, small fragments of technical and social heritage that show how the Cold War world was connected.

Above, left and below: Sections of TAT-1 cable
Images © National Museums Scotland

Above, right: Oban in Scotland where the transatlantic cable is seen being hauled ashore.
SuperStock / Alamy Stock Photo

Chapter 1

Nuclear nation

In 1964 Alexander MacIntyre of Strone designed a tartan for the personnel of the American submarine base at the Holy Loch; it was registered as 'Polaris Military' after the (in)famous nuclear-capable submarine-launched ballistic missile. The pattern includes navy blue to represent the naval uniform, dark green for the depths of the oceans, and the Royal blue and gold overchecks represent the 'Blue' and 'Gold' crews who alternate on duty on the submarines armed with the missile.

The Polaris Military tartan embodies the cultural and physical impact of the Cold War in Scotland. It visualises the elements that will be explored in this chapter: the close relationship between the military and civilian life, especially in technology; the importance of Scotland's characteristic topography; and how enmeshed the nuclear war element of the 'imaginary war' was in everyday life.[1] A fabric that reminds us of national dress, and has historically been associated with Scottish military service in the British Army, now represented Scotland as a location for a different kind of warfare.

The Cold War featured in Scottish life not only in the environs of the lochs on the Scottish west coast in which the Polaris submarines were stationed, but also more widely. Scotland's geography made it strategically critical during the four-decade nuclear stand-off between East and West. Although in Europe this Cold War never turned 'hot', there were profound consequences for those on the northern frontline.

Especially in the earlier decades of the conflict, Scotland's situation overlooking the GIUK Gap – through which Soviet vessels needed to travel to reach North America via the Atlantic – made it crucial for the United States and its allies. There were over 200 military bases and installations in Scotland at the height of the Cold War, including the high profile Royal Navy and US Navy bases on the Clyde.

Miltary tartan ties

These tartans, including the Polaris Military tartan, were commissioned by US military personnel stationed in Scotland during the Cold War. They represent the relationships that formed between Americans and their families and the Scottish communities where they were based.

Image © National Museums Scotland

Pages 24–25: Reactor Control Room at Chapelcross Nuclear Power Station, Annan, c. 1960

The control rooms at Chapelcross were central to ensuring the nuclear reactors were working safely and efficiently. Using specialist devices and equipment, workers were able to control and monitor the fuel rods and the rates of nuclear fission. By 1963, Chapelcross was producing 222 megawatts of electricity.

© Nuclear Restoration Services

Scotland's physical geography was not only important for storing weapons. It also provided ideal locations for the generation of nuclear power. By examining both nuclear weapons and nuclear power, we will show how technical developments, hopes of a bright energy future and fears of a nuclear war were linked. Scotland was – and, arguably, remains – a nuclear nation.

Nuclear dawn

On 16 July 1945, the Manhattan Project in the United States detonated an atomic device code-named Trinity in New Mexico. Beyond the immediate devastation and the characteristic mushroom cloud, Trinity sent shockwaves around the world. Many argue that the detonation marked a new geological epoch, the Anthropocene, and that it heralded the dawn of a new political age.[2] The United States then dropped atomic bombs to devastating effect at Hiroshima and Nagasaki, killing some 200,000 Japanese civilians and drawing the Second World War to a close as Japan surrendered.

Given the terrifying power of this technology, after the war the United Nations sought to centralise nuclear weapons development, but in vain. As the Iron Curtain descended, the United States closed its doors and continued to develop even more devastating devices. Soviet scientists tried to catch up, and in 1949 tested their first atomic device (dubbed 'Joe-1' by the Americans). Both superpowers then set about developing thermonuclear weapons – hydrogen bombs – that were many times more powerful than those dropped on Japan. This arms race and the resulting stockpiling of weaponry locked them into 'mutually assured destruction' (MAD) – which, in principle, would prevent either side from deploying them.

British scientists had been instrumental in the Manhattan Project. For example, Scottish physicist Samuel Curran developed an innovative method of detecting radiation; he would later return to Glasgow and serve as the first Principal of the University of Strathclyde, established in 1964. Nevertheless, after the war the Americans initially refused to co-operate further with the United Kingdom in the development of nuclear weaponry. In 1947 the British set about their own research programme, determined to be among the front-runners of the nuclear arms race.

'We've got to have this thing over here,' demanded Foreign Secretary Ernest Bevin, 'whatever it costs. We've got to have the bloody Union Jack on top of it.'[3] Sure enough, as 'Operation Hurricane', the United Kingdom detonated its first atomic device over the Monte Bello Islands, off the coast of Australia, in 1952. The Air Ministry had commissioned British companies to develop a fleet of bomber aircraft, the V-force, to drop such devices.

Massive explosions notwithstanding, much of this development was undertaken behind a veil of intense secrecy. However, there were other manifestations of atomic technology that were ostensibly less sinister: splitting the atom could be explosive in one context, but under control could generate power for peaceful purposes.

At the 1951 Festival of Britain – intended to shake off the post-war social and economic malaise and parade British success in the arts and sciences – there were nuclear motifs on everything from wallpaper to an atomic clock. Concentrated at the South Bank Centre in London, there were also festival events and displays across the country, including an indus-

Exhibition of Industrial Power, Glasgow, 1951

The 1951 Festival of Britain aimed to showcase British innovation. This sketch by Sir Basil Spence shows the proposed atomic energy display in the Exhibition of Industrial Power in Kelvin Hall, Glasgow.

© Sir Basil Spence Archive. Courtesy HES

trial show at Kelvin Hall in Glasgow and an arts exhibition in Edinburgh at the Royal Scottish Museum (now the National Museum of Scotland).[4]

The Festival was not the only evidence of wider optimism and a welcoming of the prospect of nuclear power. Nuclear energy became the source of hopes as well as fears. American President Dwight D. Eisenhower's phrase 'Atoms for Peace' echoed throughout the 1950s on both sides of the Atlantic. He wanted countries with nuclear capability to dedicate their 'strength to serve the needs rather than the fears of mankind'.[5] In particular, the potential for nuclear energy was a source of much excitement: an 'Atoms for Peace' exhibition travelled through Europe (including Glasgow) and an 'Atom Train' toured the rail network in Britain.[6]

Not only did American nuclear propaganda attract interest in Scotland, but so did Soviet technological achievements, such as the Sputnik rocket launch in 1957 and Yuri Gagarin's 1961 space flight. The 'Space Age' influenced modernist design with new products reflecting renewed faith in scientific progress. And when the international fish processing vessels known as 'Klondykers' arrived, Scottish consumers connected with their Soviet counterparts via the exchange of such goods.

Above, left: Soviet Vostok 1 launch souvenir

This desktop souvenir made in the Soviet Union commemorates the Vostok 1 launch on 12 April 1961 in which Yuri Gagarin was the first human to be launched into space. Gagarin instantly became a national hero and came to embody the triumph of the Soviet space programme.

Image © National Museums Scotland

Right: 'Orbit' patterned triangular-shaped earthenware

Showing the popularity of atomic design, this 'Orbit' pattern triangular-shaped earthenware segmented platter was designed by Peter Forster for Carlton Ware Ltd in c.1957.

Image © National Museums Scotland

This optimism especially focused on civil nuclear reactors, which promised abundant, cheap, clean energy. The United Kingdom promised to be a world leader in their development. Those parts of the country embracing this bright future would be lifted from the economic privations of the immediate post-war. This ideal, this nuclear dawn, appeared bright and cheerful.

The advent of nuclear power

After the Second World War, British industrial supremacy seemed threatened by friend and foe alike. The Government therefore threw itself into the new nuclear science, so that the United Kingdom would be at the forefront of the atomic race, as it had once led the Industrial Revolution. Scotland was key to these developments, not least because of its topography. It had lots of coastline, an abundance of lochs, and – outside the Central Belt at least – low population density.

Just south of the border, the first full-scale atomic power station in the world was Calder Hall (now Sellafield) on the Cumbrian coast. A young Queen Elizabeth II switched it on in 1956, and the facility ran until 2003. In 1958, the United Kingdom Atomic Energy Authority (UKAEA) opened a sister plant at Chapelcross on the site of an RAF aerodrome near Annan, Dumfriesshire – which was to be a new Scottish 'Atom Town'.

The first of the four reactors at Chapelcross began generating power in 1959, with the power station reaching full capacity the following year. 'We are entering the threshold of a new era,' declared local grandee Sir John Crabbe at the opening. 'It is the nuclear era. Scotland can be proud of the part she is playing in this revolution. This station is not hidden but is erected

Above: Model of Calder Hall

A model of Calder Hall in Cumbria, the United Kingdom's first Magnox nuclear power station, with dual commercial and military outputs.

Image © National Museums Scotland

Opposite: Chapelcross float in Annan's Riding of the Marches

The nuclear power station at Chapelcross enhanced the struggling harbour town of Annan, providing opportunities for well-paid and skilled employment, new schools, housing and recreational activities. Its role in the community is shown by these Chapelcross staff in the traditional Riding of the Marches celebrations.

Annandale Observer / Heritage Service, Dumfries and Galloway Council

where it can be seen for miles around and is a monument to progress and the nuclear era.'[7]

Chapelcross was ideally located, having access to established transport links and proximity to both the River Annan for plentiful water (200,000 gallons per day) and the Solway Firth for discharging effluent. It was also reasonably close to its sister site in Cumbria. To build Chapelcross, the UKAEA contracted engineers and construction workers from across Britain, as well as hiring local boiler makers and other firms. The local economy benefitted from the influx of personnel and jobs, including a strong tradition in apprenticeships; and the accompanying social infrastructure for both the incomers and locals.

For nearly half a century the four reactors and their giant cooling towers – the 'Sentinels of the Solway' – dominated the landscape. Amid doubts about its structural integrity and commercial viability, Chapelcross stopped generating electricity in 2004, and the characteristic towers were demolished in 2007.

Like Calder Hall power station, Chapelcross had Magnox reactors, so called because their uranium fuel elements were sealed in magnesium alloy cans. Nine more would follow across Britain's waterways and coasts over the next decade, as the workhorses of the British civil nuclear industry.[8]

Construction began in 1957 on Hunterston on the North Ayrshire coast to the west of Glasgow. When it opened in 1964 it was the largest of its kind

in the world and, unusually, the reactors were loaded from below; the two reactors were 10 metres above ground level.

The Hunterston facility (later joined by Hunterston B) is now considered Scotland's first *civilian* nuclear power plant. This is because Chapelcross, like Calder Hall, had another purpose. In the words of Derek Latimer, former apprentice:

> … they were producing electricity from nuclear power and this was made to be a big part of it, but really what we were producing was plutonium for the British bomb. Whether you agree with that or not that's what the thing was basically for. The electricity was simply a means of getting rid of the heat.[9]

Chapelcross' primary function was to generate weapons-grade plutonium; power output was a secondary outcome, absorbing the heat generated in the process and generating steam to power giant generators.

This was to satisfy a growing demand for fissile material to be used for nuclear weapons. After the success of the tests of 1952, British scientists developed their first operational atomic weapon, Blue Danube, first dropped in the Australian desert in 1956. The intended stockpile of these and successor devices demanded quantities of plutonium that Calder Hall and Chapelcross were to supply. The nuclear industry, from which Scotland continues to draw power (at the time of writing), is an artefact of the Cold War.

Above: Chapelcross nuclear power station

Before their demolition in 2007, the cooling towers of Chapelcross could be seen for miles around. These towers were a symbol of Dumfriesshire's connection to the Cold War.

Tom Kidd / Alamy Stock Photo

Opposite: Hunterston mimic panel

In 1964, the Hunterston nuclear power station in North Ayrshire officially opened with two Magnox reactors capable of generating 180 megawatts of electricity. This control panel with its analogue controls shows the contemporary aesthetic of the design.

Image © National Museums Scotland

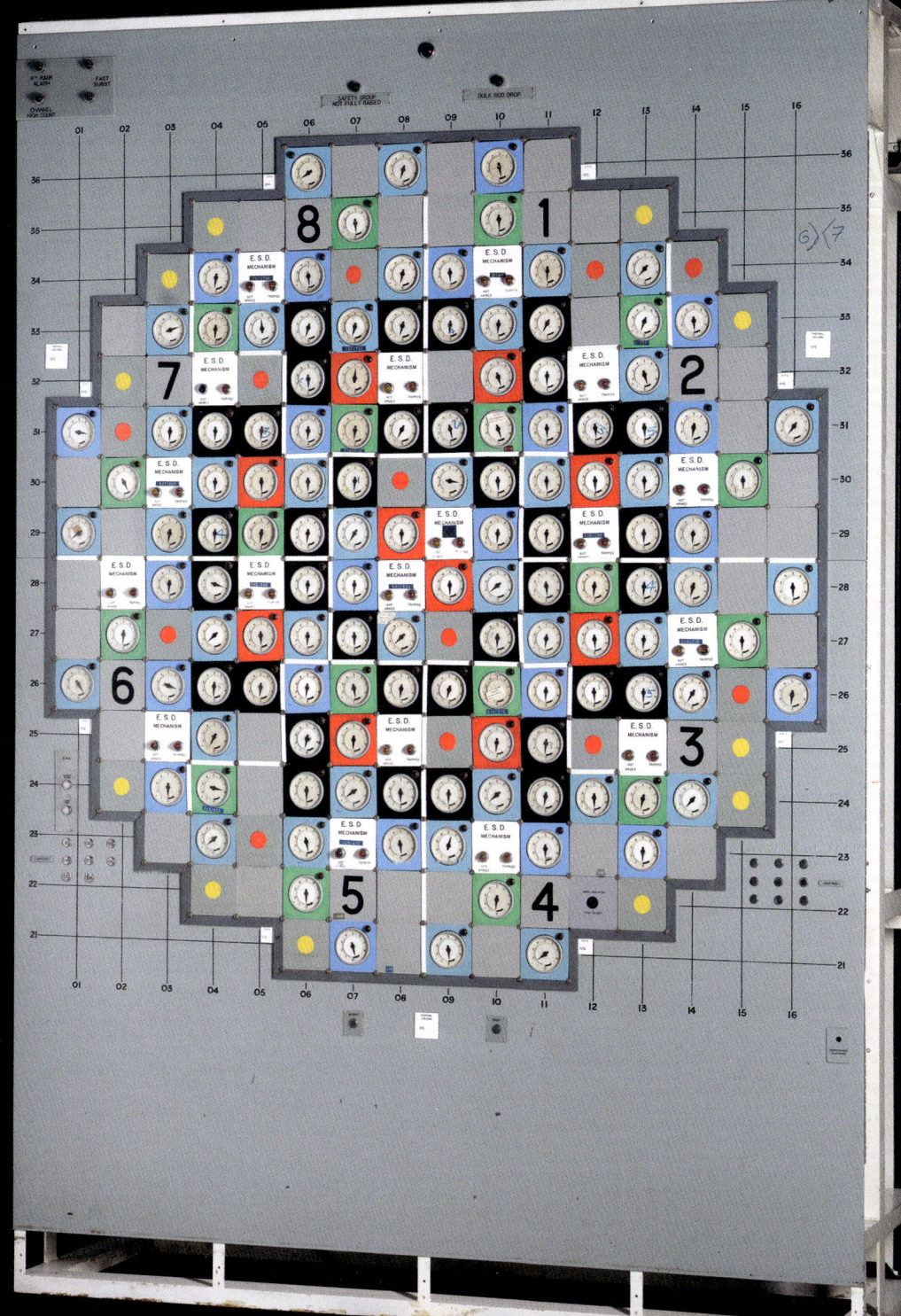

The Americans arrive

Aircraft-borne nuclear weapons were not to endure, however. Even as the V-force bombers were taking flight, it was clear they would not serve effectively as a deterrent. Free-falling nuclear devices could not deter intercontinental ballistic missiles, and Blue Danube or other atomic weapons were dwarfed by the new generation of thermonuclear devices. Moreover, new technology meant that the bombers carrying nuclear weapons could be easily intercepted. Airborne threats alone would not suffice, and the nuclear powers prepared to submerge their nuclear threats.

The US Navy had already, in 1954, launched the first submarine powered by a small nuclear reactor which produced the steam that propelled the vehicle and allowed the generation of clean air. It was named USS *Nautilus* after the vessel in Jules Verne's *Twenty Thousand Leagues Under the Sea*. Unlike diesel-electric submarines (termed 'boats' in naval circles) used during and since the Second World War, *Nautilus* could cover large distances at high speed and only needed to surface to pick up consumables.

To get the best out of submarines, however, the United States needed to find a base for them that was closer to the Soviet Union (not to mention further from the United States). The Soviet Navy was enhancing its fleet and flexing its muscles, so the perceived seaborne threat was growing. A base in Northern Europe would suit the Americans well.

Accordingly, in 1959 President Eisenhower asked the British Prime Minister Harold Macmillan for a location in Scotland – somewhere relatively close in European terms to North America for communications and sea or air travel, and with strategic access to the GIUK Gap and the expanse of the North-East Atlantic.

At the time, Macmillan wanted to convince the United States to sell the Skybolt airborne missile system to the United Kingdom to arm the V-force, as the British alternative, Blue Streak, had been cancelled due to spiralling costs. Eisenhower was agreeable to the suggestion, in return for a site for American nuclear submarines. Macmillan made no precise promise, but mentioned the Clyde as a potential area.

Macmillan would later be evasive when pushed on the specific location, and the UK Admiralty assessed other sites including Invergordon on the Cromarty Firth in North East Scotland, Milford Haven in Wales, and the established naval base at Falmouth in the far south-west of England. There were also two options further north on the Scottish west coast, at Loch Linnhe or Loch Ewe – but they were too far from established transport links for the Americans.[10] In the end, the UK Government grudgingly agreed to a base on the Holy Loch in Argyll, code-named while in development 'Lamachus' (after the ancient Athenian general).

The Holy Loch was ideal for American purposes as it fed into the Firth of Clyde and was protected from, but accessible to, the Irish Sea. The US military was familiar with it, having undertaken training exercises there during the Second World War, and it was close to Prestwick airfield which had been reactivated for American use in 1951. Prestwick was a former Second World War transatlantic ferry flight terminal, which would be critical for the Holy Loch base for personnel and supplies.

Over the course of the Cold War they expanded their presence in ports (including Greenock and Rosyth), air bases (such as Campbeltown and Stornoway, where atomic weapons were stockpiled), navigation stations (Thurso and Shetland), and in firing ranges, logistics and intelligence bases.

The activities of the growing Soviet Navy and its nuclear submarine fleet were monitored from the large electronic intelligence base at Edzell in Angus.[11] In 1960, the US Navy moved into this former First and Second World War British airstrip (and sometime motor-racing circuit) to set up the Naval Security Group Oceanographic Monitoring Station. Some 3000 civilian, military and intelligence staff served there, although precisely how many and who they were is still unknown. At various times it included a code-breaking training facility and a pioneering satellite technology, White Cloud, which used heat signatures to identify ships. The Americans would retain a presence at Edzell for 37 years.

The Holy Loch was also a relatively short distance from the airstrip at Machrihanish on the west coast of Argyll, which would serve as a large NATO fuel depot as well as a potential nuclear weapons store. Machrihanish had the longest runway in Scotland at the time and could be used by the V-force bombers. But the bombers' days were numbered: the United States had, in the meantime, successfully tested a nuclear missile, Polaris, that was sufficiently powerful and small enough – a mere 28 feet and 14 tonnes – to be fired from a submarine. These would be at the heart of the American presence.

The Cold War arrived in Scotland on 3 March 1961 as USS *Proteus* sailed up the Holy Loch. Scotland was now at the centre of the frontline of the nuclear deterrent. *Proteus* was a Second World War vessel adapted as the refit ship for the submarines, as the US Navy did not feel confident enough to build a base on land. A left-wing UK Government might reverse the commitment to host the submarines, and there had been sufficient local resistance for the authorities to persuade the Americans to arrive on a work day, Friday 3 March, when protestors were less likely to attend *Proteus*' arrival.

Even so, there was local Labour Party support for the base because it brought significant economic benefits, such as jobs to support its 3000 personnel. A young George Robertson, later NATO Secretary General, watched as the first American submarine arrived. He later reflected: 'The arrival of the Americans in the Holy Loch was a huge happening in Scottish and even international terms, but in its human impact it was most marked on those in the Cowal locality.'[12]

USS *Patrick Henry*, the first armed Polaris submarine, arrived five days after *Proteus*. It was the first of a fleet to be stationed at the Holy Loch, with three at base at any one time. *Proteus* would later be replaced by the bespoke tender USS *Hunley*, and the base would be extended to accommodate four boats at one time. *Hunley* was followed by the vast floating dry dock USS *Los Alamos*, whose 150-metre, 19,000-tonne bulk dominated the coastline.

As discussed in the Introduction to this book, Scotland's place as a Cold War battleground was chillingly emphasised the following year during the Cuban Missile Crisis. As the Americans and Soviets escalated the tension, not only were the RAF's Vulcan bombers loaded up with their nuclear payload, but also all six submarines, as well as USS *Proteus*, were at sail with firing orders in the Norwegian Sea, Barents Sea and the Eastern Mediterranean. Such was the urgency with which *Proteus* set sail, one eyewitness recalls seeing crew running along the side of the ship, cutting all shore fastenings and communication cables with an axe.[13]

A Soviet trawler, stationed off the west coast to monitor submarine activity, may or may not have detected them. It is known that the facility at Edzell, meanwhile, played such an important role in gathering data that the US Senate considered it to have been 'performing a mission vital to the security of the nation'.[14] Fortunately, the then American President John F. Kennedy and Soviet Premier Nikita Khrushchev were able to defuse the conflict, the submarines' dread orders were never issued, and regular patrolling recommenced. But the crisis served to confirm the British direction of travel towards a maritime deterrent.

Dounreay powers up

The United Kingdom continued its efforts to improve its own independent nuclear capability. The Magnox reactors were not particularly efficient in generating either plutonium or grid power, so British scientists and officials decided to experiment with a more effective 'fast' reactor, and set out to find a site. With plentiful water and few settlements close by, in 1954 the Government selected the former RAF airstrip at Dounreay on the north coast of Caithness.[15]

Dounreay was as far from Whitehall on the British mainland as possible. The same site had been considered for American Thor missiles, which in the end were stationed in English RAF bases.[16] It was also close to the former signals intelligence station at Thurso, which would be switched back on in 1962 to assist the Polaris fleet.

Dounreay would house three civilian reactors.[17] The main experimental reactor, and the first to be constructed, was the famous Dounreay Fast Reactor, active between 1959 and 1977. This was in the iconic 40-metre steel sphere, built by Motherwell Bridge Company to minimise the spread of radioactivity in the event of accidental release. Meanwhile, the Dounreay Materials Test Reactor had commenced its construction and would go on to test different fuels and the behaviour of materials from 1958 until 1969. The Prototype Fast Reactor was then in operation from 1974 until 1994. Dounreay's principal function was to test these new technologies, but over the course of its active life the facility also supplied some power to the grid.

The massive workforce at Dounreay comprised not only locals, but also specialist experts brought in for their technical skills known as the Atomics. 'You felt you were a part of something,' remembered Willie Sloss, a metallurgist from Glasgow who moved there – 'and it was new, exciting.'[18] Power was not the only impact of Dounreay, which changed the economic and social shape of northern Scotland. It was itself part of the large-scale post-war infrastructure investment that involved a huge increase in public expenditure in Scotland.[19]

USS *Patrick Henry* in the Holy Loch

The 6700-ton American Polaris submarine *Patrick Henry* joined USS *Proteus* in the Holy Loch in 1961 and would conduct 17 deterrent patrols from Scotland.

Keystone Press / Alamy Stock Photo

Opposite, above: USS *Proteus* in the Holy Loch

The USS *Proteus*, a submarine tender ship, arrived at the Holy Loch in March 1961 to service the nuclear submarines equipped with Polaris missiles. *Proteus* set sail during the Cuban Missile Crisis to support the activated submarines.

Trinity Mirror / Mirrorpix / Alamy Stock Photo

Opposite, below: USS *Los Alamos* at the Holy Loch

USS *Los Alamos* also joined the fleet at the Holy Loch. This vessel was an advanced section base dock – in effect a floating drydock – used to service the US Polaris submarines.

NB/ROD / Alamy Stock Photo

Dounreay nuclear power station

The Dounreay experimental nuclear facility perched on the north coast of Scotland.

© Nuclear Decommissioning Authority (NDA)

Willie Ross, the Secretary of State for Scotland who was to welcome Soviet Premier Alexei Kosygin to Hunterston (see pages 97, 100), was determined to bring Prime Minister Harold Wilson's 'white heat of technology' to Scotland. By generating employment-based migration northwards, Dounreay reversed Caithness' post-war population decline.[20]

The site changed the face of Thurso. The town's population tripled in size as 2800 Atomics arrived in 1958 alone. To the locals and those who made their lives on the north coast, Dounreay was a long-term and stable source of jobs. As one local farmer reflected:

> ... when it was announced ... the new fast breeder reactor was to be situated at Dounreay ... it caused immense excitement in those days up here, because people knew very little about that way of life. It came in at a very fortunate time for Caithness, because the agricultural industry was running down its need for labour and many people who were farm workers moved to work at Dounreay or moved to work for building contractors and it provided a great fill-up in the employment market ... . Well I think the people, it was Caithness people, were welcoming it and they were delighted to see employment coming to the county. It certainly did that.[21]

Especially welcome were the opportunities to develop highly technical skills. These came with their own particular risks and staff were ever-vigilant about the dangers of radiation. 'You always had your film badge with you and had a special monitoring device that was attached to you,' recalled one operative. 'This was read each time you came out and recorded on your records as to what radiation you had collected.'[22]

Dounreay soon became part of the fabric of everyday civilian life in Caithness. However, the explicitly military element of the Cold War was never far away. Looming large next door was the Dounreay Submarine Prototype, a facility for testing and developing nuclear submarine capacity. The Ministry of Defence had commissioned engineering giant Rolls-Royce to lead a consortium to undertake the Herculean task of developing British nuclear propulsion technology.[23]

The mission was to follow the Americans in manufacturing a nuclear reactor – similar to those in civilian power plants, but at a fraction of the size and robust enough to share a confined space with crew for prolonged periods. This involved a reactor using pressurised water that would not only power the engine and electricity but also generate clean water and oxygen for the crew.

Construction began in 1957 on the Admiralty Reactor Test Establishment, to be dubbed HMS *Vulcan* (reiterating the Navy's practice of naming its land facilities as if they were ships). As well as testing nuclear reactor technology, Vulcan was a site for developing and maintaining seagoing equipment and training submarine engineers, including a Naval Training Simulator which replicated a manoeuvring room in a submarine.

PWR1, the first of two pressurised water reactors (PWR), started operations in 1965 and continued to evolve until it shut down in 1984. By this time naval training had ceased, but a new PWR was under construction at Barrow-in-Furness, on the north-west coast of England, for operation at Vulcan. It travelled 500 miles around the coast by barge, then skated the final mile overland, at the time the largest load carried over the longest distance in Britain. At the heart of a new Shore Test Facility, PWR2 commenced in 1987, and, with a number of different cores, this would run until 2015.

This technical development and the close relationship between military and civilian aspects of the operation did not always run smoothly. Already in the construction phase, a key decision to use an alloy alternative instead of stainless steel proved unwise as flaws appeared in the material, impacting both the developing nuclear plant and the nuclear submarines (see below). Only by going cap-in-hand to the forceful head of the US nuclear submarine programme, Vice Admiral Hyman Rickover, was the Royal Navy able to get the programmes back on track.[24]

Rickover, who had visited Dounreay himself during one of his argumentative visits to Britain, used the situation as leverage to ensure the use of the Holy Loch and freedom from what he saw as interference on the site by the British. The provision of American parts also meant that the Dounreay plant was not quite as purely British as its Government had hoped during a strained period in relations between the two countries.

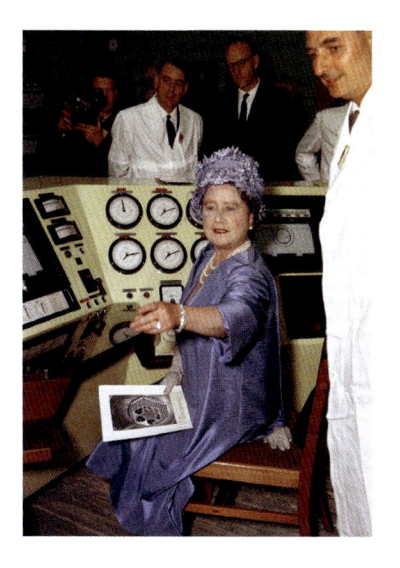

Royal visitor to Dounreay

Throughout the Cold War, Dounreay welcomed key politicians, public figures and royalty to view the positive developments in nuclear energy. Her Majesty the Queen Mother is pictured here on her second visit to Dounreay in August 1961.

© Nuclear Decommissioning Authority (NDA)

Atomic Scotland – Dounreay

In the 1950s, harnessing the power of nuclear energy was a priority for the UK Government. The 1955 White Paper *A Programme for Nuclear Power* outlined the development of an experimental 'fast-breeder' reactor to be sited at Dounreay on the north coast of Scotland. This kind of reactor was intended to generate more nuclear fuel than it consumed thanks to the fissile reaction at its core.

Over fifty years of operation, three nuclear reactors were constructed onsite, each more technologically advanced than the last: the Dounreay Materials Test Reactor, the Dounreay Fast Reactor, and the Prototype Fast Reactor. In 2007, the Nuclear Decommissioning Authority began the long process of decommissioning Dounreay.

During the decommissioning there has been close attention to preserving the heritage of this unique site. National Museums Scotland has played a role as a member of the Dounreay Heritage Advisory Panel and by acquiring objects from the site. The collection includes control room panels, safety and measuring equipment, and (non-radioactive) fuel elements. In 2007, the Museum purchased Kate Williams' uranium glass sculpture of the iconic sphere that surrounded the Dounreay Fast Reactor. The green glow comes from ultraviolet underlighting. This piece incorporates not only the technical achievements associated with Dounreay but also continuing concerns surrounding radioactivity.

Opposite, above: Sculpture of Dounreay Power Station, Kate Williams, 2007

Image © National Museums Scotland

Opposite, below: *Eagle* comic, Vol. 8 No. 42, featuring Dounreay Fast Reactor

Reproduced by kind permission of the Dan Dare Corporation Limited – www.dandare.com

Above: Isotope calculator

Image © National Museums Scotland

Below: Dosimeter and charging unit used at Dounreay

Image © National Museums Scotland

41

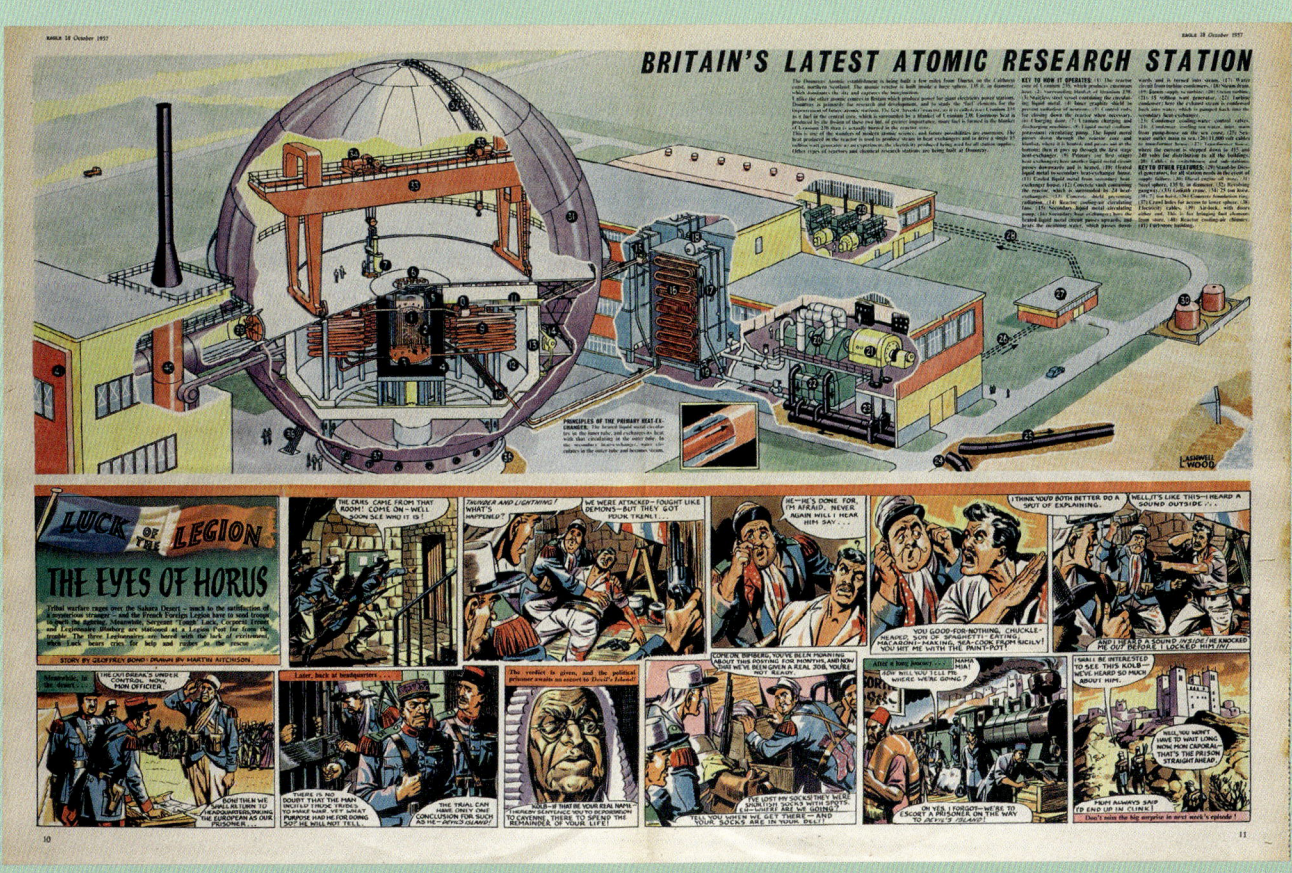

The British Polaris

Welcome or not, co-operation with the Americans was key to the development of British nuclear weapons. While the United States had stationed its own nuclear-powered and nuclear-equipped submarine on the Holy Loch, the United Kingdom still lacked a nuclear weapon that could deter the Soviet Union. Long-range nuclear missiles, without the need for aircraft, were becoming the gold standard in nuclear weaponry, rendering the RAF nuclear bombers obsolete.

And so, even as the V-force were taking to the skies, the UK Government was already planning its replacement. Like the Americans, the British sought answers beneath the waves. As an effective deterrent, the prospect of submarine-launched missiles had distinct advantages over airborne solutions. As a circulating fleet on perpetual patrol, they were difficult to discern in the deep ocean compared to even the highest, fastest bombers.

On Trafalgar Day, 21 October 1960, Queen Elizabeth II launched the first British nuclear-powered submarine at Barrow-in-Furness; but because the British technology was not yet developed, HMS *Dreadnought* sported an American-made engine. *Dreadnought* was a hunter-killer, designed to track down other submarines. It would take a further three years to be ready for service. But as well as nuclear-*powered* boats, the United Kingdom in due course would want them nuclear-*armed*.

This shift towards a sea-based deterrent was driven at least as much by the relationship between the United Kingdom and the United States as by internal British strategic considerations. In December 1962, to Prime Minister Harold Macmillan's dismay, the Americans unilaterally cancelled the development of the Skybolt missiles which were supposed to have saved the V-force from the scrapyard. Determined to maintain the 'special relationship' between the two countries, Macmillan met the American President, John F. Kennedy, just before Christmas at Nassau in the Bahamas.

The United Kingdom's reliance on Skybolt, now off the table, effectively gave the British no choice but to move to a marine deterrent. Under the terms of the Nassau Agreement announced in April 1963, the United States reluctantly agreed to sell their Polaris missiles to the British. Harold Wilson, who as Leader of the Opposition had objected to Polaris, changed his mind after he was elected Prime Minister in 1964. By this time the Ministry of Defence was well underway building the warheads and the boats to carry them.

Leading the Polaris Executive for the Royal Navy from New Year's Day 1963 was a Scot, Rear Admiral (later Sir) Hugh 'Rufus' Mackenzie.[25] Born in Inverness, Mackenzie had been a submariner since 1935 and commanded four boats throughout the Second World War, including a 12,000-mile patrol, the longest of any British submarine during the war. After teaching on the notoriously difficult Perisher submarine commander course after the war, he visited USS *Nautilus* during a visit to the United States as a staff officer. The Polaris programme Mackenzie oversaw would become the largest fixed-term industrial undertaking in British history at a cost of £370 million (over £6.5 billion in today's terms).

The British Polaris programme involved the development of four 'Resolution' class submarines long enough to carry the Polaris missiles. These evolved beyond reliance on American engines and, instead, Mackenzie opted for a reactor based on the PWR development at Vulcan. Crews of the first two, the original HMS *Resolution* (launched in September

1966) and HMS *Repulse* were trained in the United States until a British training school was operational; engineers also had training at Dounreay. HMS *Renown* and HMS *Revenge* completed the set. HMS *Resolution* first went on active patrol in June 1968 and all four were operational by the end of the following year. The British nuclear deterrent had formally submerged.

The facilities aboard these vessels for their 13 officers and over 130 other personnel were somewhat better than other submarines, but they needed to be: crews spent up to 60 days at sea, almost entirely cut off from sending any communication. Indeed, few on board knew precisely where they were. One of the pre-arranged ways they would know if the worst had happened was if Radio 4's 'Today' programme was not aired.[26] Such clandestine operations, however, were effective: it was later claimed that no British Polaris submarine was detected at sea by the Soviets.[27] Rather, in Mackenzie's words, their threat hung like the 'Sword of Damocles'.[28]

These new vessels required a new base. After fierce deliberation, the Government decided that western Scotland would host this deadly deterrent alongside its American counterpart. The waterways west of Glasgow had important qualities that made them attractive for hosting the British nuclear submarine deterrent, just as they had appealed to the Americans, with multiple exit routes and active shipping lanes to hide the submarine traffic. The Royal Navy wanted a major conurbation at a safe distance, but nevertheless accessible by land. The base would also need to be on water deep enough for submarines to submerge in any harbour.

The Admiralty considered Rosyth and Plymouth, but ultimately decided on the former Second World War submarine base at Faslane on the Gare Loch, which had housed the 3rd Submarine Squadron since 1957. The loch is one of the jagged waterways adjoining the upper Firth of Clyde, secluded but with swift access to the North Atlantic, and 30 miles north-west of Glasgow.

In March 1968, HMS *Neptune* – as the Clyde submarine base at Faslane was formally named – officially opened after five years of preparation, £25 million investment and up to 2000 workers on-site at its peak. This was in spite of the 'Great Glasgow Storm' that battered the west coast that January, damaging not only the site but also 250,000 houses.

Existing berths had been adapted to be the docks for the nuclear and conventional submarines, frigates, and for a massive floating dock. They also constructed engineering facilities, administration and accommodation. These would then be staffed by over 3000 service personnel, and almost as many civilians by the 1970s. Outside its gates, the base would also attract an ongoing protest that was to become the longest-running peace camp in Britain.

The Faslane base would need an accompanying support facility to store and maintain the warheads, detonators and torpedoes, as well as other armaments and equipment. It needed to be less than an hour away by water, but no closer than 4400 feet as the crow flies (and radiation spread) for safety.

After a site at Glen Douglas was considered and discounted, the Royal Naval Armaments Depot was situated at Coulport on Loch Long, the extensive waterway between the Holy Loch (and the US base) and the Gare Loch (with the British submarines). Loch Long's steep banks required some adaptation of the facilities, but otherwise it was well suited. Coulport is eight miles by road and 13 miles by sea from Faslane; the Holy Loch's proximity was actually more of a disadvantage because of the risk of attack or accident.

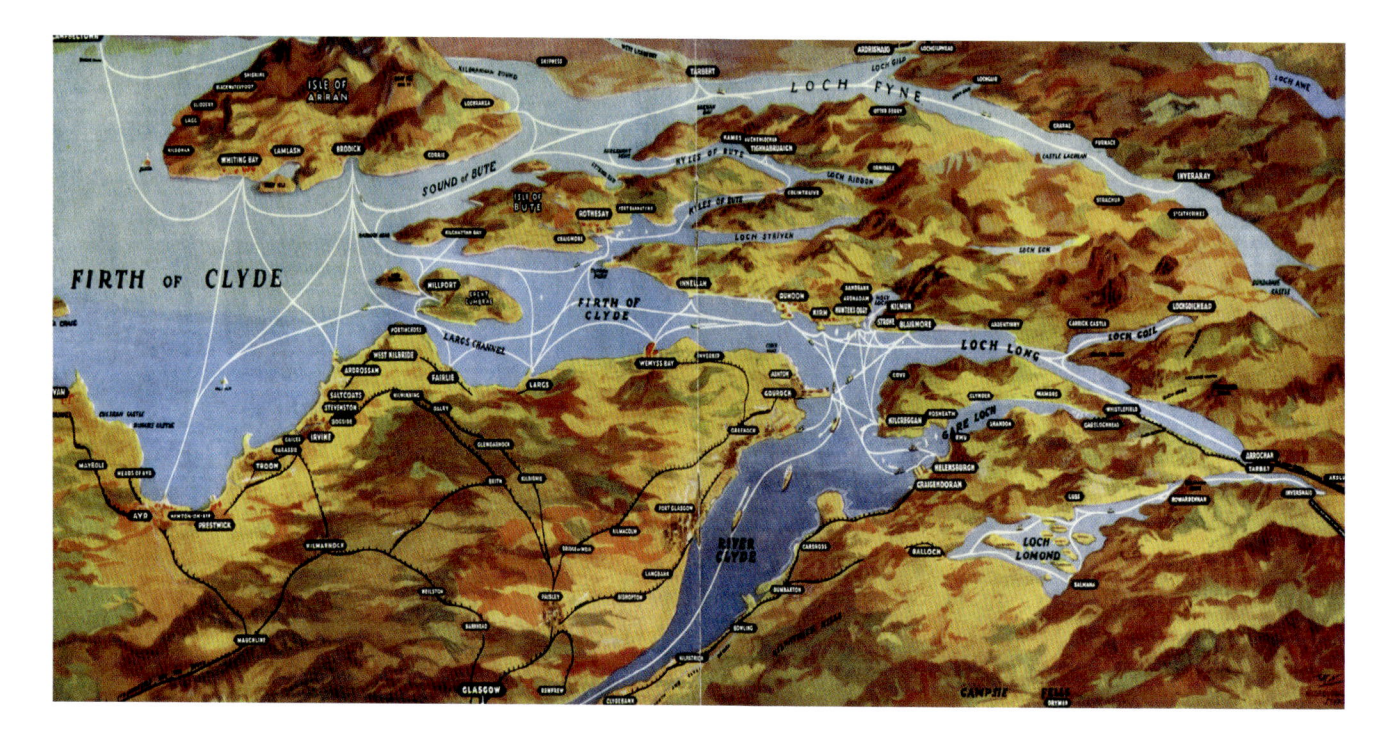

One further element of the required infrastructure remained: a Royal Navy facility to refit and refuel the nuclear boats. In 1962, the Government announced that Rosyth was to be used for this purpose. Although barely more than ten miles west across the Firth of Forth from Edinburgh, Rosyth was deemed far enough from a major population centre to be appropriate. In 1968, *Dreadnought* was the first to come in.

However, even as the Polaris boats were being deployed, work on a new generation of nuclear weapons was beginning. The Ministry of Defence was keenly aware that anti-ballistic developments enabled the Soviet Union to shoot down Polaris missiles, thereby weakening their effect as a deterrent.

Initially, the UK Government and its scientists at the Atomic Weapons Research Establishment in Aldermaston, along with other Government research agencies, embarked on a top-secret project to develop its own improvement to Polaris, albeit with some American input. The Chevaline system was intended to improve Polaris missiles in such a way that they could evade any anti-ballistic missiles used by the Soviet Union. But the Chevaline project was soon called into question as the United States began to develop a new generation of submarine-launched missiles called Trident.

The economics of Trident would become politically divisive, but the impact of nuclear infrastructure was already being felt. Like the Holy Loch and Dounreay, the military installations linked to the nuclear deterrent at Faslane, Coulport and Rosyth had significant economic and social effects, while environmental impacts – especially around uranium mining – were a growing issue for the anti-nuclear movement.

Firth of Clyde landscape, *c*.1951

This map from a *Festival of Britain* booklet, shows the geography and topography of the Firth of Clyde and the surrounding lochs which would become home to both British and American nuclear submarines from the 1960s onwards.

Glasgow City Archives

Opposite: British Nuclear Targets, *c*.1972

This page is from a previously 'top secret' document written by the Ministry of Defence which outlines 'Probable Nuclear Targets in the United Kingdom'. The document notes down key military and strategic locations which may have been vulnerable to a nuclear attack.

The National Archives, ref. DEFE11/646

TOP SECRET

ANNEX A TO
COS 1311/2/5/72

PROBABLE NUCLEAR TARGETS IN THE UNITED KINGDOM: ASSUMPTIONS FOR PLANNING

Note: Figures in brackets denote total targets in each category

1. TARGETS RELATED TO ALLIED NUCLEAR STRIKE CAPABILITY (67)
a. CENTRES OF CONTROL ETC (21)

  i. Government - Central (2)   Central London
                                Cheltenham

     - ex-Regional (12)   Catterick   )
                                York   )   These are
                                Preston   )   considered to be
                                Cambridge   )   possible, rather
                                Dover   )   than probable
                                Reading   ) former RSG) targets
                                Salcombe   ) sites
                                Brecon   )
                                Kidderminster)
                                Armagh   )
                                Edinburgh   )   See also
                                Nottingham   )   paragraph 2

  ii. Military - Maritime (4)   Northwood (HQ, CINCHAN/CINCEASTLANT)
                                Plymouth (HQ, COMCENTLANT)
                                Pitreavie (HQ, COMNORLANT)
                                Fort Southwick (HQ, C-in-C Naval Home Command)

      - Air (3)   High Wycombe (HQ, Strike Command)
                                Ruislip (HQ, 3rd US Air Force)
                                Bawtry (HQ, 1(Bomber) Group, Strike Command)

b. BOMBER BASES (including dispersal
   recovery and flight-refuelling
   bases) (33)

  i. RAF (22)   Scampton
                                Waddington
                                Honington
                                Wittering
                                Marham
                                Coningsby
                                Lossiemouth
                                Finningley
                                Bedford
                                Kinloss +
                                Manston +
                                Wattisham +
                                Cottesmore
                                Wyton
                                St Mawgan +
                                Machrihanish +
                                Leeming +
                                Valley +
                                Brawdy +
                                Coltishall +
                                Yeovilton +
                                Leuchars +

+ Dispersals at these stations have been temporarily de-activated and
  HQ Strike Command will give 3 months notice of intention to re-activate.

TOP SECRET

Despite such concerns, after initial scepticism as to whether an equivalent base in England would have been situated so close to a major city, local politicians welcomed the economic investment, and the combination of the British and US navies off the Firth of Clyde changed the local area significantly. In the 1960s, the Royal Navy put more effort into providing married quarters and family life in its bases, including Faslane and Coulport, so the personnel brought ready-made communities with them, with considerable buying power.

However, not all of the local employment promised in the planning of these bases materialised, and the highly specialised staff often arrived from elsewhere. Although the bases would change the local social landscape, they would also attract passionate communities of protesters. The shining nuclear age was losing its lustre.

Torness protest poster, 1979

The Scottish Campaign to Resist the Atomic Menace (SCRAM) led the opposition to the construction of Torness nuclear power station in East Lothian, organising protests to highlight the dangers of nuclear energy and to halt progress on the site.

Image © National Museums Scotland

Central Scotland nuclear blast map, c. 1980s

This map of central Scotland has been colourfully annotated to depict the potential devastation caused by a nuclear attack. The concentric circles, plotted on possible Soviet targets, show the effect of a bomb from ground zero to the spread of nuclear fallout carried by wind across the country.

Image © National Museums Scotland

Nuclear dusk

Early atomic optimism faded as the nuclear energy revolution failed to live up to its early promise and transform British life. Apart from the two initial Magnox reactors, Scotland housed only one further nuclear power facility, at Torness, east of Edinburgh. Its eight-year construction commenced in 1980, to considerably more disquiet than its predecessors. It aroused the particular ire of the Scottish Campaign to Resist the Atomic Menace (SCRAM), founded in 1976.

Among SCRAM's arguments were concerns about the disposing of nuclear waste, and that Torness would contribute to the 'plutonium economy' and thereby exacerbate the nuclear weapon stockpile.[29] As well as organising a protest – during which thousands of protesters occupied the Torness site – and further acts of civil disobedience in South East Scotland, SCRAM also widened its concerns to oppose nuclear power in general and organise further sizeable anti-nuclear demonstrations.

The realities of being a Cold War nuclear frontline became part of the Scottish lived experience in other ways too. From the decision to accommodate the American submarine base at the Holy Loch, Scotland's extra security also clearly made it a potential target for proactive attacks or a nuclear retaliation.

This was not mere fantasy. The Soviet authorities had a detailed understanding of Scottish geography. Not only were the Clydeside bases of interest, but so were other elements of civilian and military infrastructure.[30] It is now known that the radar station at Saxa Vord on Unst, for example, would have been a possible target for a three-megaton bomb.

Had the Forth and Clyde been targeted by nuclear weapons early in the Cold War, as was likely, over 50,000 and nearly 100,000 people respectively would have perished.[31] In the era of thermonuclear weapons, given the location of populations and military infrastructure, the whole Central Belt and much of Scotland's coastline and north islands would have been targeted to devastating effect. Watchfulness, readiness and the mobilisation of Scottish society and infrastructure were all ways to manage the apprehension that such a prospect generated (see Chapter 2).

Even though there was no full-scale nuclear confrontation, there were other risks involved in storing and maintaining nuclear weaponry. Submarines and nuclear boats would occasionally snag fishing nets, at times with fatal consequences. The Americans, it later transpired, suffered a number of accidents in Scotland.

In 1970, three personnel died in a fire on the Polaris tender ship USS *Canopus* on the Holy Loch. It was fortunate that the fire did not spread to the two nuclear submarines that were docked alongside.[32] Four years later, and even more alarmingly, the nuclear-powered and armed submarine *James Madison*, upon exiting the Holy Loch, collided with a Soviet submarine waiting to take up its trail. Both boats surfaced and, mercifully electing not to engage, submerged again.[33]

In 1981, also at the Holy Loch, a crane operator dropped a Poseidon missile around 14 feet while transferring it to the tender ship USS *Holland*. Although the warheads would not have been set off, the radiation would still have spread; in the event the safety brake prevented anything worse.[34]

British boats were not without their accidents. HMS *Renown* was particularly troublesome, colliding with a merchant ship in the Irish Sea in 1969 and hitting the bottom off the Scottish coast while on sea trials in 1974.[35]

Chapelcross fire, 11 May 1967

After noticing abnormal levels of carbon dioxide, workers discovered a fire in one of the Chapelcross reactors caused by a melted Magnox can. Senior staff (shown here from left to right: Dr J. H. Martin, Mr L. Clark and Mr D. MacDougall), were tasked with removing the blockage by going behind the biological shield wearing inflated PVC suits.

Annadale Observer / Heritage Service, Dumfries and Galloway Council

Nuclear electricity generation for the grid came with its own risks too. Scotland, thankfully, avoided accidents on the scale of those suffered close by in 1957 at Windscale (near the original Calder Hall station in Cumbria), and farther afield at Three Mile Island in the United States in 1979 or, most devastatingly, at Chernobyl in Ukraine in 1986.[36] In May 1967, however, there had been a fire in one of the Chapelcross reactors due to a blocked channel after a Magnox can melted.[37] Operatives shut down the reactor immediately and three senior members of staff entered the reactor in pressurised PVC suits to clear the blockage. They were successful – the excess radioactivity was contained within the reactor – but Reactor 2 shut down for two years.

More consequentially, it later transpired that in 1977 there had been an explosion in a shaft on the Dounreay site used for waste disposal. In the early hours of 10 May, a Vulcan security officer noticed a cloud heading seaward from the neighbouring site; a Dounreay security operative then found glass and concrete strewn around the head of the shaft. Some two kilograms of sodium and potassium had reacted with water and blown the five-tonne concrete lid off, scattering radioactive particles over a wide area.[38] The shaft had been used since 1959, and small particles from the original Material Testing Reactor's fuel elements spread to the local beaches. 'As a precaution,' notes health advice to this day, 'the harvesting of seafood is prohibited within a two-kilometre radius of a point near Dounreay.'[39]

Beyond the Cold War

Not all of these accidents were known at the time, and for a spell in the 1970s there appeared to be reasons to be hopeful. The global situation seemed to hold more promise. International relationships thawed as the United States and the Soviet Union considered arms control during a decade of détente.

In 1979, however, the Soviet Union invaded Afghanistan. By the early 1980s, with Conservative Margaret Thatcher in Downing Street and Republican Ronald Reagan in the White House, many feared that the threat of nuclear war – and the threat posed by the US military in Scotland – seemed as present as ever. The Americans were replacing Polaris with Poseidon missiles with a longer range; and although they withdrew submarines from Europe, they retained the Holy Loch base because of its strategic proximity to the GIUK Gap.

The United Kingdom also remained committed to a nuclear deterrent. Against the backdrop of the heightened international tensions of the 1980s, Chapelcross (by this time run by British Nuclear Fuels Ltd, which had broken off from the UKAEA) began to generate tritium for hydrogen bombs.[40] During the construction of the plant for this process, for the first time Annan attracted significant protest from nuclear activists including SCRAM.[41]

Even though Mikhail Gorbachev embarked on a more peaceful Soviet foreign policy after he came to power in 1985, leading to a key Intermediate-Range Nuclear Forces Treaty in 1987, the United Kingdom was already committed to a new generation of submarine-launched missiles. The previous Prime Minister, James Callaghan, and American President Jimmy Carter had committed to the new Trident missiles to replace Polaris before the 1979 election that brought Margaret Thatcher to power.

Aware of the importance of connections to the United States, the Royal Navy had always been sceptical of the UK-driven Chevaline project, and the Admiralty lobbied actively and successfully for the American system. The Thatcher Government announced the purchase of Trident I in 1980. This decision was then reversed and an order for the new Trident II system was announced in 1982.

Trident required much larger boats, so in 1986 new Vanguard submarines were planned to replace the 'Resolution' class submarines. Faslane and Coulport had a £1.9 billion upgrade and Rosyth a £220 million reconstruction. Yet by the time HMS *Vanguard* arrived in 1992, the Berlin Wall had fallen and the Soviet Union had been disbanded. Even the Americans had departed the Holy Loch (Trident having a long enough range to remove the need for a European submarine base altogether). The first submarine patrols with Trident missiles only began in 1994, almost five years after the Cold War had ended. Polaris was in use until 1996.

The United Kingdom and the United States had not based nuclear weapons in Scotland to fight a nuclear war with the Soviet Union, but rather, in principle, to prevent one. Even so, the end of the Cold War did not spell the end of nuclear weapons, nor of nuclear power in Scotland. The country was irrevocably changed; and so were its people.

Notes

1. Matthew Grant and Benjamin Ziemann (eds), *Understanding the Imaginary War: Culture, Thought and Nuclear Conflict* (Manchester: Manchester University Press, 2016).
2. The Anthropocene Epoch is an unofficial unit of geologic time, used to describe the most recent period in Earth's history when human activity started to have a significant impact on the planet's climate and ecosystems. From https://education.nationalgeographic.org/resource/anthropocene/.
3. A 1947 meeting later remembered by Michael Perrin on BBC *Timewatch*, 29 September 1982.
4. *Report for the Year 1951 on the Royal Scottish Museum* (Edinburgh: Scottish Education Department, 1952).
5. Dwight D. Eisenhower, 'Atoms for Peace', 8 December 1953, www.iaea.org/about/history/atoms-for-peace-speech.
6. Alison Boyle, '"Banishing the atom pile bogy": Exhibiting Britain's first nuclear reactor', *Centaurus* 61 (2019), pp. 14–32.
7. Newsreel quoted in Sarah A. Harper, *Chapelcross and the Cold War: Scotland's First Nuclear Power Station* (Eastriggs: Devil's Porridge Museum, 2018), p. 14.
8. Simon Taylor, *The Fall and Rise of Nuclear Power in Britain: A History* (Cambridge: UIT Cambridge, 2016).
9. Quoted in Harper, *Chapelcross and the Cold War*, p. 11.
10. Peter Hennessy and James Jinks, *The Silent Deep: The Royal Navy Submarine Service since 1945* (London: Allen Lane, 2015).
11. Trevor Royle, *Facing the Bear: Scotland and the Cold War* (Edinburgh: Birlinn, 2019).
12. Quoted in Andrene Messersmith, *The American Years: Dunoon and the US Navy*, 2nd edn (Edinburgh: Argyll Publishing, 2023), p. 7.
13. 'The Cuban Missile Crisis', podcast episode 28 July 2020, https://whatwedointhewinter.com.
14. Quoted in David G. Mackay, 'Scotland: The United States strategic footprint during the Cold War', 2019, https://digital.nls.uk/1980s.
15. Stephen Cashmore, 'Caithness– Dounreay', 1998, www.caithnessarchives.org.uk/dounreay.
16. Brian Lavery, *Shield of Empire: The Royal Navy and Scotland* (Edinburgh: Birlinn: 2007).
17. William A. Paterson, *50 Years of Dounreay* (Wick: North of Scotland Newspapers, 2008).
18. Willie Sloss, Jimmy Simpson and David Crowe, interview with James Gunn, 13 March 2014. Dounreay Memories Oral History Project.
19. T. M. Devine, *The Scottish Nation: A Modern History*, new edn (London: Penguin, 2012).
20. Linda M. Ross, 'Dounreay: Creating the Nuclear North', *Scottish Historical Review* 100 (2021), 82–108.
21. John Young, interview with James Gunn, 6 March 2013. Dounreay Memories Oral History Project.
22. John Macrae, interview with James Gunn, 6 February 2013. Dounreay Memories Oral History Project.
23. *The History of the Vulcan Naval Reactor Test Establishment Dounreay* (Thurso: Rolls-Royce, 2007).
24. Hennessy and Jinks, *The Silent Deep*.
25. Hugh Mackenzie, *The Sword of Damocles: Some Memories of Vice Admiral Sir Hugh Mackenzie* (Gosport: Royal Navy Submarine Museum, 1995).
26. Royle, *Facing the Bear*.
27. Lavery, *Shield of Empire*.
28. Mackenzie, *The Sword of Damocles*.
29. Scottish Campaign to Resist the Atomic Menace, *Torness Nuclear Power Station: From Folly to Fiasco* (Edinburgh: SCRAM, 1983).
30. John Davies and Alexander J. Kent, *The Red Atlas: How the Soviet Union Secretly Mapped the World* (Chicago: Chicago University Press, 2017).
31. UK Government estimates in 1953, in Royle, *Facing the Bear*.
32. '2 Prisoners and Guard Died In Fire on Polaris Tender', *New York Times*, 30 November 1970.
33. Matthew Weaver, 'Scottish cold war nuclear submarine collision kept secret for 43 years', *The Guardian*, 25 January 2017.
34. Royle, *Facing the Bear*.
35. Jim Ring, *We Come Unseen: The Untold Story of Britain's Cold War Submariners* (London: John Murray, 2003).
36. Serhii Plokhy, *Atoms and Ashes: A Global History of Nuclear Disasters* (New York: Norton, 2022).
37. 'Efficient Organization the Keynote at Chapelcross: Chapelcross Scientists First in Scotland to Enter a Reactor', *Annandale Observer*, 26 May 1967.
38. Rob Edwards, 'Lid blown off Dounreay's lethal secret', *New Scientist*, 24 June 1995.
39. Corporate Report, 'Monitoring of beaches near Dounreay information leaflet', updated 30 April 2024, https://www.gov.uk/government/publications/onshore-monitoring-of-radioactive-particles/information-leaflet-about-the-monitoring-of-beaches-near-dounreay.
40. Rob Edwards, 'Never mind the tritium, watch the plutonium', *New Scientist*, 20 May 1995.
41. 'CND Mount Tritium Protest', *Annandale Observer*, 25 August 1978.

BRITAIN
YANKE
CLOSE ALL U.S. BASES IN BRITAIN
CLOSE ALL U.S. BASES IN BRITAIN
CLOSE ALL U.S. BASES IN BRITAIN
CLOSE ALL U.S. BASES IN BRITAIN
BOMBERS HOME
SCOTS SAY NO! -TO- US BASES
MAKE BRIT SA NO U.S. BASES HERE
I want to live

COME AS FRIENDS BUT LEAVE YOUR ROCKETS AT HOME
MAKES
H-BOM
TARGET

Chapter 2

Mobilising Scotland

On 23 June 1959, a crofter on South Uist, an island in the Outer Hebrides off the west coast of Scotland, saw 'a most beautiful thing to watch'.[1] He had just observed the launch of a Corporal missile, a weapon that could carry nuclear warheads, being tested by the US military from the Royal Artillery Guided Weapons Range on the island. The crofter's experience shows how the Cold War not only affected cities but also rural areas. It also highlights how Cold War mobilisations were related to wonder as much as fear.

Chapter 1 looked at how the Cold War in Scotland involved the mobilisation of nuclear technology that could be harnessed for military and civilian uses in the Cold War competition; but it also meant the mobilisation of society more broadly. Wars are fundamentally about mobilising people and *matériel* – that is, military equipment and supplies needed to fight wars – for specific objectives. This chapter seeks to demonstrate how mobilisation during the Cold War changed – and was influenced by – Scottish society, economy, culture and politics. The extent of the military mobilisation of Scottish society might not have been visible to everyone at the time, as its specific shape was often kept secret.

To understand these mobilisations and their relationship to Scottish life, we will explore the geography of Scotland and the locations of Cold War infrastructure. Then we will touch on the economic impact of the conflict and Scots' involvement in military and civilian uniformed services. Finally, we will assess the particular role of religion in Scottish life and its relationship with the peace movement, rounding out the varied and often conflicting attitudes to the clash of superpowers.

Mapping and monitoring

Wars involve the control and knowledge of territory, and the Ordnance Survey mapping of Great Britain since the eighteenth century was in fact a military exercise.

Pages 52–53: March on RAF Edzell, 1960

Scottish people mobilised to oppose the positioning of American nuclear weapons in Scotland and to show their concerns about Scotland becoming a Soviet target. This march on RAF Edzell shows the Scottish flag on the leading banner and other signs protesting against the site.

Image © National Museums Scotland

Opposites: Soviet map of East Lothian, c. 1985

The Soviet Union created highly detailed maps of areas across Scotland such as this one of a section of East Lothian. These maps highlighted the topography of the landscape including hills, rivers, and green spaces as well as marking key roads, towns, and villages.

Image © National Museums Scotland

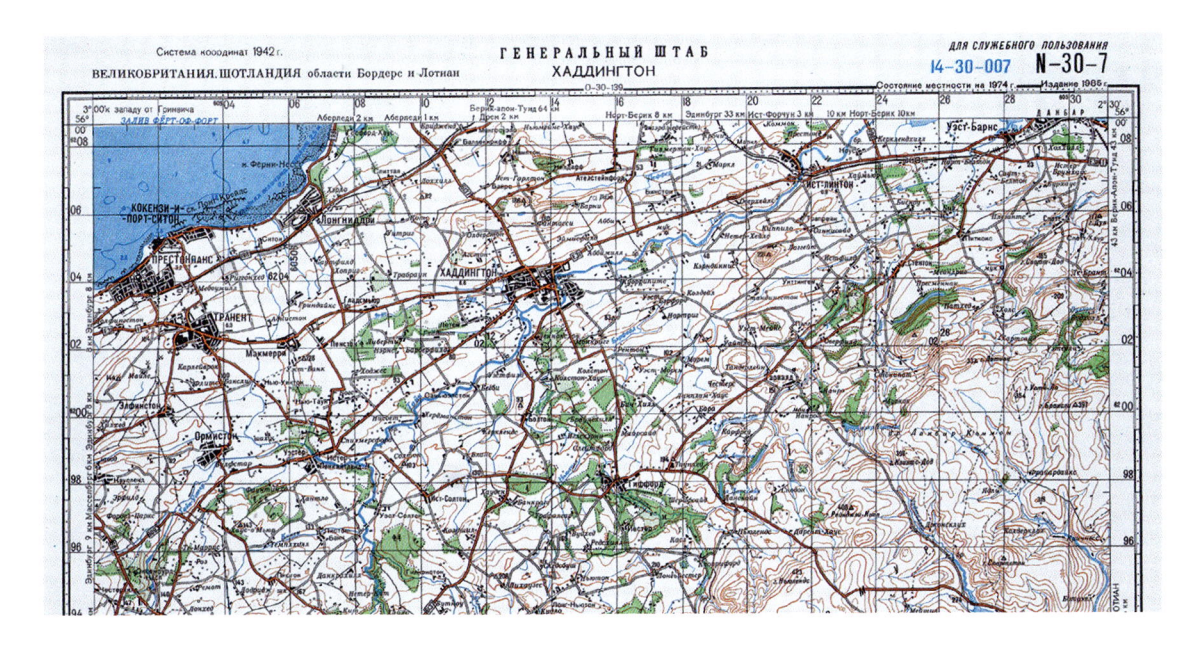

Maps offer a fascinating perspective on the Cold War in Scotland and illustrate how the boundary between war and peace at that time was never clear-cut. Maps, such as those that were part of a programme first launched by the Soviet leader Joseph Stalin, mapped civilian places across the world, but their main purpose was the potential control of territory during wartime. From the 1960s, much of their information was gathered by analysing data from remote sensing via satellites, but people also collected data on location, often under the pretence of scientific research.

To the Soviet Union, Scotland appeared, from a bird's-eye view, as a strategic geographical location on a map. Soviet military maps – like their Western counterparts – contained plenty of information that a civilian map at the time did not. Soviet cartographers colour-coded key public buildings and factories, as well as noting street names, post offices and even bus stops on their maps.

The National Library of Scotland in Edinburgh has collected some of these Soviet maps. They look like the type used in Britain at the time by tourists or other visitors, but the Soviet maps showed the streets and sites in Cyrillic script. Some even revealed features not shown by Ordnance Survey maps, such as the details of sites relevant for international or domestic security.

For Edinburgh, for example, a 1983 Soviet map revealed details of the footprint of Saughton Prison – information that did not appear in the Ordnance Survey map at that time. Others showed the width of smaller roads in new building developments, or the depth of the Clyde in Glasgow, the Forth-Clyde Canal or the River Forth. There was also information on obsolete military infrastructure, such as disused airfields.[2] Through such maps, we get a sense of what the peace activist Malcolm Spaven called 'Fortress Scotland'.[3]

While similar maps were held within the Ministry of Defence in London and other Government agencies, most Scots at the time were probably oblivious to the extent to which

Лист 2
БАЛГОУНИ-ХАУС
БРИДЖ-ОФ-ДОН
Дон
ОЛД-АБЕРДИН
БУХТА АБЕРДИН
НОРТ-КЕРКХИЛЛ
ИСТ-КЕРКХИЛЛ
ТОРРИ
БУХТА НИГГ
Норт-Лойрстон
Лойрстон
Берибанкс
1:10000
1:10 000 Абердин (О-30-104) на 2 л. Лист 2 СЕКРЕТНО 1981 г.

The Royal Navy Air Station, Crail, Fife

In 1956, the Joint Services School for Linguists opened in Crail, Fife, to teach languages such as Russian, Czech and Polish to those on their National Service. The emphasis on teaching Russian came from the need to monitor and understand Soviet military communications.

© Crown Copyright: HES

Opposite: Soviet map of Aberdeen, c. 1978

This Soviet military map of Aberdeen demonstrates the attention to military sites across Scotland. These maps also contained key data on industrial sites and other locations which did not normally appear on publicly available maps in the UK.

Reproduced with the permission of the National Library of Scotland

Scotland had been fortified, and certainly unaware of the extent of the massive bases discussed in the Introduction. People knew about installations in their local area, or had heard rumours about Government bunkers, but they had little confirmation. Ironically, it was the peace activists, in the 1980s, who created more public knowledge of this form of military mobilisation by systematically mapping and interpreting military sites.

These maps reveal a more general characteristic of Cold War mobilisation that is also relevant for the mobilisation of other parts of society. Scotland's Cold War cannot be understood unless we look back to at least the Second World War, as most of the basic installations, such as navy bases, airfields and radar posts, have their origins in that war, or in the run-up towards it.

The Royal Naval Air Station in Crail in Fife, for example, was commissioned in 1940, but then used to house a cipher school that offered Russian language training to soldiers in the 1950s. When it was eventually put on the market in 1962, potential buyers included a geriatric hospital, a bulk food storage company and Caledonia Egg Producers Ltd.[4]

The initial military mobilisation of Scottish infrastructure for the Cold War did not start in 1945 (with the end of the Second World War) or in 1947 (with the Marshall Plan, an assistance programme by the United States to strengthen Europe economically against the Soviet Union), or in 1949 (with the foundation of NATO). It began in earnest after a series of crises, not least the building of the Berlin Wall in 1961 and the Cuban Missile Crisis in 1962.

Apart from the arrival of US nuclear submarines on the Holy Loch and British nuclear submarines close by in Faslane and Coulport, this period of the Cold War saw the redevelopment in Scotland of already existing bases and airfields at Prestwick, Lossiemouth, Stornoway and Machrihanish. Naval fuel depots at Campbeltown, Loch Striven and other locations were constructed, as well as the large dishes for microwave antennae in Shetland that were part of NATO's ACE (Allied Command Europe) system.

Military infrastructure had important repercussions for civilian life. The new Marconi surveillance radar at Saxa Vord – intended to enable secure communication between NATO allies – brought electricity with it, enabling features of modern life such as a cinema to come to the island.[5]

In addition to new technology, the United Kingdom relied on volunteers to help with surveillance. As part of the secret UK-wide 'Operation Hornbeam' during the 1970s, fishermen from Aberdeen operating in the Barents Sea were asked to report Soviet vessels to a contact at the Ministry of Defence.

More visible and widespread, however, was the role of the Royal Observer Corps (ROC) in civil defence. The ROC, set up in 1925 to monitor the skies above Britain, involved 27,000 volunteers during the Second World War. Having been stood down in 1945, it was remobilised in 1947 and repurposed during the Cold War to spot Soviet bombers and measure radioactivity in case of an attack. However, the advent of radar made the ROC more or less redundant in spotting aircraft, and its main role switched to preparation for nuclear attacks.

From 1957, ROC volunteers worked with the United Kingdom Warning and Monitoring Organisation (UKWMO), under the control of the Home Office. Their key task was to provide the Government with information about the scale of a nuclear attack. In 1968, the civil defence programme was abandoned, apparently no longer useful as the threat had shifted from nuclear bombs dropped by plane to much faster nuclear missiles. Civil defence volunteers continued to serve, however, until the 1990s.

Although the ROC was probably of limited tactical importance, its history tells us a lot about how the British imagined a nuclear war to unfold – and about the plans required to control it. The Cold War expansion of the network of ROC underground monitoring posts was part of an effort to spread defence infrastructure away from the cities and large urban areas into the countryside.

A Government report in 1955, the Strath Report, had argued that cities offered poor protection in a nuclear war and that the nuclear radiation from hydrogen bombs was so strong it would drift into the countryside as well. The key challenge for defence dispersal, therefore, was to build bunkers and monitoring stations that would be located away from major cities, but offer protection from this radiation.

Another surprising element of this dispersal away from urban centres was the Government's leasing to ferry company David MacBrayne of three purpose-built ships complete with nuclear-safe blast doors. In the event of nuclear war, they were supposed to ferry supplies, banknotes and gold bullion around the United Kingdom.[6]

Royal Observer Corps Post, Traquair, Scottish Borders

Royal Observer Corps volunteers routinely practiced setting up their underground monitoring posts. After preparing the equipment above ground, Observers would close the hatch and descend the 4.5-metre ladder into the small operations room ready to respond to a potential nuclear attack.

Sarah Harper

In the 1960s, the United States expanded its military presence on the Scottish east coast, by turning the newly built RAF Mormond Hill in rural Aberdeenshire into an important centre for command, control and communication activities. British installations were regularly leased to the US armed forces, and Scotland became part of what one critic called the 'international web of US presence overseas'.[7]

Scotland's varied terrain – long coastlines as well as hills and mountains – offered a popular site for military training for both British and NATO forces. In 1991, just after the end of the Cold War, the army used Scotland for 208,000 training days per year.[8] There was a firing range at Cape Wrath, for example, and the mountain terrain of the Highlands offered ideal conditions for infantry instruction. Because of its relatively clear airspace, the Royal Air Force used Scotland at various points for flying exercises.

There were also more disturbing uses of remote Scotland. Until the middle of the 1950s, the sea west of the Isle of Lewis was used for biological weapons testing, conducted in absolute secrecy. In autumn 1952 HMS *Ben Lomond*, along with a survey boat, set anchor in a bay around 20 miles north of the island's capital Stornoway. Scientists from the Royal Navy, as well as the Chemical and Biological Defence Establishment, conducted experiments on board using guinea pigs and monkeys.

Furthermore, in 'Operation Cauldron' the UK Government conducted tests during which they released bubonic plague bacteria into the air. A trawler, *Carella*, from Fleetwood in Lancashire and on its way to Iceland, ignored the warnings and inadvertently passed through the cloud of plague bacteria. The Royal Navy did not intervene at the time, apart from monitoring the ship's movements and listening for any health distress signals. Fortunately, none of the 18-man trawler's crew was infected.[9]

The Royal Observer Corps (ROC)

The Royal Observer Corps (ROC) was stood down after the Second World War but was reactivated in 1947 in response to growing tensions with the Soviet Union. The ROC prepared for and would report on nuclear attacks from 1560 underground monitoring posts across the United Kingdom.

These small posts, four metres below ground, housed specialist monitoring and communications equipment as well as furniture and domestic items for the Observers. When called to action, or while practising, Observers would descend by ladder into the post which contained two small rooms: a chemical toilet cupboard and an operations room.

Observers were issued with equipment such as the Bomb Power Indicator and Ground Zero Indicator to measure the distance from ground zero, and the size and yield of nuclear devices, which they would report back to their designated Group Headquarters.

Fortunately, such devices were never needed and after the Cold War ended the ROC disbanded. Since stand-down, there have been efforts to restore monitoring posts and preserve the objects used in them. The National Museum of Flight holds the contents of an ROC post, donated from the Edinburgh Group Headquarters shortly after stand-down.

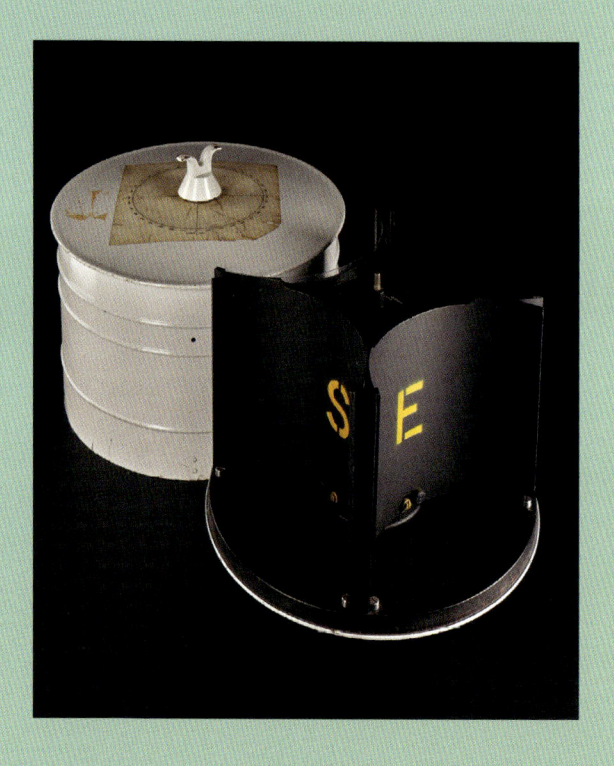

Above: Ground Zero Indicator

Image © National Museums Scotland

Opposite, top: Model of a Royal Observer Corps underground monitoring post

Image © National Museums Scotland

Above, left: Bomb Power Indicator

Image © National Museums Scotland

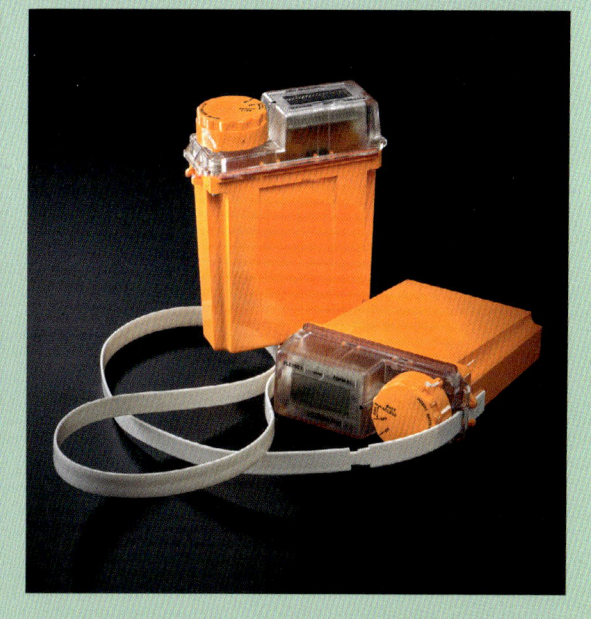

Above, right: Fixed post and personal Dose Rate Meters

Image © National Museums Scotland

The 'warfare state'

During the Second World War, the UK Government had orientated a great proportion of economic activity towards weapons and ordnance production. There was no wartime economy in Scotland during the Cold War at this scale, but still the state played an active role in shaping the economy between 1945 and the 1970s. The historian David Edgerton has called this the British 'warfare state'. He observes that the Government had 'intimate links with business, and indeed it successfully intervened in the economy, transforming … industrial structure'.[10]

The mobilisation of industry and manufacturing also involved research and development. Some historians of technology have even argued that 'the history of military science and technology can be seen as recounting campaigns of the Cold War, as much as actual military engagements constitute the campaigns of hot war'.[11]

This mobilisation of the Cold War economy – the links between specific private companies and Government – had taken shape already over the course of the 1930s and continued up until the privatisations initiated by Conservative Governments in the 1980s. It is thereby possible to trace the history of the 'warfare state' in Cold War Scotland by looking at employment patterns and at specific sites.

For example, the Royal Ordnance Factory in Bishopton near Glasgow, with its roots in the two world wars, employed around 3000 people to produce explosives by the late 1970s. When the factory was privatised in 1984 and sold to British Aerospace, the plant still had a workforce of around 2000.[12]

Military installations such as airfields also had sizeable civilian workforces (such as accountants, secretaries and administrators). Together the combined personnel at such installations played a major role in the local economy. In 1950, there were 1950 service personnel and 280 civilian workers at RAF Kinloss on the Scottish east coast. This was equivalent to 40 per cent of the local labour force in the area.[13]

Following the massive mobilisation of the economy during the Second World War, Scotland became a key site for Britain's defence-industrial complex. In particular it profited from the defence investment that followed the Korean War of 1950–53.

Initially, the reputation of Scottish workers as being especially radical, and the memory of the strikes and unrest of 'Red Clydeside' in the wake of the First World War, appear to have worked against locating a new defence industry in Scotland. A manager at Rolls-Royce complained that the area was 'seething with communists and strikes and threats of strikes occur the whole time'; while another stated that 'Clydeside workers are the most difficult in the world to handle'.[14] Nonetheless, Clydeside remained a major area for building warships, manufacturing naval ordnance and for naval engineering more generally.

There was also increased investment by aerospace industries in central Scotland starting in the early 1940s, but this was primarily by companies whose headquarters were based elsewhere, such as Rolls-Royce Engines in Hillington, Ferranti in Edinburgh or Scottish Aviation Limited Ltd in Prestwick.

Ferranti became one of the leading military electronics companies in the United Kingdom over the course of the 1940s and 1950s, working primarily on optical equipment such as gyroscopes for guns, bombs and missiles. Barr & Stroud in Glasgow, which had been involved in the production of naval range finders since the late nineteenth century, also became a major player in electro-optical defence equipment in the 1950s.

Even though, by the following decade, Ferranti, Barr & Stroud, Rolls-Royce, the shipbuilder Yarrow in Clydeside and the Rosyth Dockyard in Fife had consolidated their positions as the main defence contractors in Scotland, there were other players[15] – between 1962 and 1978 Scott of Greenock, for example, built almost half of the total order of 27 new diesel-electric submarines for the Royal Navy.[16]

Defence funding shielded the defence-related sector in Scotland against the deindustrialisation noted in other areas such as civilian shipbuilding since the 1970s. While employment in manufacturing in Scotland contracted by over 50 per cent between 1966 and 1987, work opportunities in defence and defence-related industries grew or remained at least stable.[17] In 1986, when the quasi-governmental structure of the defence sector in Scotland ended with privatisation, around 16,000 people were employed in it.[18]

Mobilisation for defence purposes also had wider economic consequences, with a significant impact on contractors and subcontractors as well as a wider ecosystem of support. Ferranti expanded from one factory in 1943 to twelve locations in 1964, which included an airstrip and a dedicated hangar at Edinburgh's Turnhouse Airport. This meant that Ferranti's workforce grew significantly, from a mere 300 workers in 1947 to 5400 in 1965 and 7500 by 1981.

Ferranti developed the AI-23 radar used in the Lightning aircraft, the Blue Parrot strike radar, the Inertial Navigation and Attack System for the Harrier and Phantom aircraft, as well as terrain-following radar for Concorde.[19]

Ferranti's expansion during the 1960s was mainly due to the company's participation

AI-23 Airborne Interception radar and test stand

In the 1950s, Scottish engineers from Ferranti Ltd developed the AIRPASS (Airborne Interception Radar and Pilot Attack Sight System) also known as AI-23 for the English Electric Lightning aircraft. This radar set aided in tracking targets more effectively at supersonic speeds. It was the first high power radar with monopulse tracking in the world to be used in squadron service. The AI-23 radar technology was used until the 1980s.

Image © National Museums Scotland

in the pan-European project to develop a new combat aircraft, the Tornado. Ferranti had been contracted to develop and build the new plane's avionics.

By attracting electronics engineers to the local labour market and by supporting local subcontractors and suppliers, Ferranti's expansion played a major role in the civilian electronics industry in central Scotland, an area that, with a nod towards Silicon Valley in California, came to be known as Silicon Glen. Hewlett Packard's branch in South Queensferry, which designed and built electronic testing equipment for export, was the most prominent of these. The dockyard at Rosyth underwent a similar process of expansion, in particular when it gained the contract for servicing and refit of the new fleet of nuclear submarines in the 1960s.

Research and development did not remain restricted to manufacturing. For example, the Phonetics Department at the University of Edinburgh received Government funding from the Ministry of Supply in the late 1950s to develop an artificial talking device. While the specific military uses remain unknown, experiments revolved around making the transmission of signals in telephone lines more effective and discussing how speech could be converted into electric waves, both tasks that were relevant for encryption.

When the Labour politician Denis Healey, as Secretary of Defence, encouraged the establishment of Higher Defence Studies at British universities in the late 1960s, John Erickson was one of the academics recruited at the University of Edinburgh. Erickson was to play a major role in research on arms control and helped to set up a dialogue between Western and Soviet academics and military officers during the 1980s, which came to be known as the Edinburgh Conversations (see pages 100–3).

Even the discovery and extraction of oil off the Scottish North Sea coast from the late 1960s onwards had a Cold War component. By the 1960s, oil and gas had replaced coal as the most important sources of energy, a direct result of the significant expansion of the motor vehicle industry generally and car ownership in particular. Oil was also an important source for manufacturing plastic – which, like private cars, was an indicator of the growth of the consumer society.

The political situation in Latin America and the Middle East, where most of the oil and gas used in the West had come from, had made deliveries increasingly insecure. Domestic sources of oil and gas, such as those discovered in the North Sea, were therefore regarded as key components of energy security. This attracted interest, especially from American investors. The infrastructure built around oil on the Scottish east coast, and the affluence it brought, thoroughly transformed that part of Scotland.

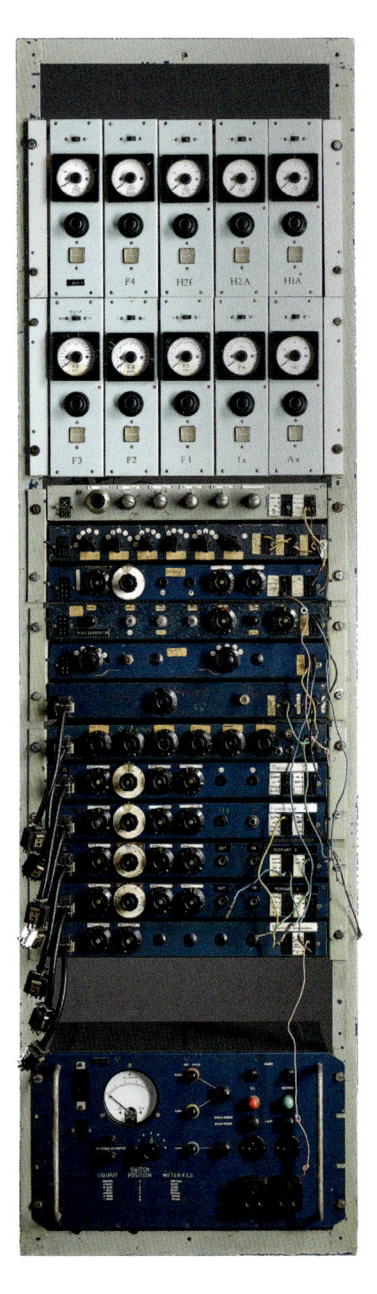

Parametric Artificial Talker

The Parametric Artificial Talker, or PAT, was developed by the University of Edinburgh in the 1950s. PAT was one of the first computers to generate human sounds artificially, rather than using recorded speech. Elements of this technology might have been used to reduce bandwidth for the Transatlantic Telephone Cable (TAT-1).

Image © National Museums Scotland

Hewlett Packard factory at South Queensferry

Hewlett-Packard was an early resident of Silicon Glen, opening a facility at South Queensferry near Edinburgh in 1965. This site specialised in designing and manufacturing telecommunications test equipment. Other key companies in Silicon Glen included Ferranti, IBM, Honeywell and Marconi.

© The Scotsman Publications. Licensor www.SCRAN.ac.uk

Mobilising people

The Cold War not only involved the mobilisation and production of *matériel*. It also meant the mobilisation of people. Most visibly, this meant the continuation of conscription from the Second World War into the Cold War.

The United Kingdom had been more reluctant than other European countries to draft young men for military service, so the introduction of National Service in peacetime was truly remarkable. Over two million men in Britain – most of them born between 1928 and 1939 – served as conscripts in the armed forces for one to two years in the period between 1945 and May 1963.

The aim was to have a readily trained large force in place in case of a land war against the Soviet Union for control of Germany. Indirectly, the draft also served as a recruitment tool for the regular armed forces since a fair number of conscripts decided to join the regular army as professional soldiers – who were often treated better than reluctant conscription soldiers. The Territorial Army, a reserve force, relied on former conscripts for its recruitment.

The Korean War had initially strengthened the sense of urgency in favour of conscription. However, with the shift towards relying on nuclear deterrence in the late 1950s, and the emphasis of technology over machines in Minister of Defence Duncan Sandys' review in 1957, it was decided to phase out conscription. The British military was also withdrawing from overseas as imperial duties reduced. The last draftees were called up in 1960.

Many of the Scots who were drafted served abroad, in particular in the British occupation forces in West Germany, but also further afield such as Korea, Cyprus, Malaya and Kenya. The majority of Scottish servicemen, however, were deployed in England. In terms of their experiences, 'national service raised questions about what the word "national" might mean in Britain', since most conceived of their distinct identities within the United Kingdom.[20]

While no one, apart from the incapacitated, was excluded from National Service, some draftees objected, citing their conscience. One of these was the son of the writer Christopher Grieve (whom we will encounter under his pen name Hugh MacDiarmid in the next chapter). In his objection, Michael argued, in addition to moral reasons of conscience, that 'national service [was] contrary to the Act of Union'. His appeal was rejected however, as the 'tribunal believed that he would be willing to fight against England'.[21] Normally, conscientious objectors cited moral or Christian pacifist motivations – or a socialist belief in not fighting against their fellow workers. Grieve's reference to the constitutional context was not common, and it is likely that it was viewed with a dose of scepticism at the time.

Apart from the boredom of drill and basic military training, many Scots, especially working-class men, were likely to have felt rather alien in predominantly English settings. Rightly or wrongly, Glaswegians had a particular reputation for rowdiness with the military authorities. There is also evidence that English soldiers often found the Glaswegian accent incomprehensible and that, as a result, Scots from Glasgow felt isolated when they served in units dominated by Englishmen.[22]

Scotsmen were also much less likely to be commissioned as officers than men from England – a fact the army itself explained by what they regarded as the inferiority of the Scottish education system and, in particular, the lack of suitable privately educated candidates.

Interestingly, however, for those who were commissioned, Scottish accents do not appear to have disadvantaged officer candidates in ways that English regional accents did.[23]

As well as those in National Service, professional soldiers from Scotland also remained highly mobilised during the Cold War. Due to Scotland's relatively small population, Scottish regiments had traditionally recruited wherever they could find recruits, whether within the populous Central Belt or outside Scotland, so that they were rarely purely Scottish. Nonetheless, Scots were over-represented in relation to the size of the Scottish population in the British Army overall.

The mobilisation of Scottish soldiers during the Cold War built upon the fearsome reputation the Scottish regiments had enjoyed. This reputation was celebrated within British imperial culture and was related to ideas about Scottish history and identity. From this perspective, Scottish soldiers were portrayed as a uniquely strong and brave bulwark in the fight against communism in Europe and across the world.[24]

There was, consequently, little debate about the participation of Scottish soldiers in the Korean War and the suppression of the uprisings in Malaya after 1951 and in Kenya in 1952. The United Kingdom's failed military operation in 1956, together with France and Israel, which tried to reclaim the nationalised Suez Canal back from Egypt, had also found support in the Scottish press. Scotland, therefore, differed little in public opinion from other parts of the United Kingdom.

The perception of Scottish soldiers also illustrates the ways in which the Cold War at home, military interventions abroad and decolonisation were connected. The image of the brave Scottish soldier fighting communism abroad remained in place until the late 1960s, when the United Kingdom withdrew from an active military presence east of the Suez Canal. When the Argyll and Sutherland Highlanders retook Crater in 'Operation Stirling Castle' during the Aden campaign in July 1967, Lieutenant Colonel Colin Campbell 'Mad Mitch' Mitchell adopted traditions of previous colonial campaigns by having the town occupied to the tune of the regimental pipes. This 'last battle of the British Empire' attracted a significant degree of mostly positive public attention at the time.[25]

Local patriotism about regiments was especially pronounced in Scotland, although the regiments often spent little time there, being based abroad. Changes to the regimental structure decreed by the Ministry of Defence in London as part of its general Cold War strategy were controversial.

When, in 1957, the Ministry of Defence announced a merger of the Highland Light Infantry and the Royal Scots Fusiliers, this was met with fierce local opposition.[26] While the Ministry of Defence regarded the merger as a relatively simple administrative act that followed the move towards nuclear deterrence as the main plank of British strategy, local protests asserted that it made no sense to merge the completely different Lowland and Highland military traditions.

There were similar debates in 1968 about the regimental merger of the Queen's Own Cameron Highlanders with the Seaforth Highlanders, and the proposal to disband the Argyll and Sutherland Highlanders who had just returned from Aden.[27] Some historians have argued that, by the early 1970s, the old regimental system based on regions had been more or less abandoned. Nonetheless, the Ministry of Defence still took account of local and national sentiment in its defence planning.[28]

God, politics and the Cold War

Myths about Scottish military prowess were part of a wider political culture that embedded Cold War ideas in Scotland. Over the course of the 1950s and 1960s, the welfare state began to replace the Empire and Commonwealth as a key marker for British as well as Scottish national identity. The Cold War reinforced this. State intervention to protect the health and welfare of citizens was a key insurance policy against communism: the stronger and healthier society was domestically, so the argument ran, the better society could defend itself against communism.

The labour movement also lost much of the radicalism that had characterised it during the 1920s and 1930s. Unlike during the First and Second World Wars, the growth of a more affluent society throughout the 1950s and 1960s promoted the integration of the working class into the rest of Scottish society. This move to moderation is exemplified by the career of the Labour politician John McGovern, Member of Parliament for Shettleston. On the Labour left, he had advocated for radical social change in the 1930s, including reducing the status of the British monarchy. In the 1950s, however, he joined the Moral Rearmament Movement to fight against 'godless Communism'.[29]

Similarly, the Scottish section of the Communist Party of Great Britain, though remaining stronger than in the rest of the United Kingdom, lost much of its influence within the labour movement, and membership and militancy declined steadily during the Cold War. Its reputation had suffered a severe blow with the official acknowledgement of Stalin's purges by the Soviet Union's leader Nikita Khrushchev in 1956.[30] During the 1930s, the Communist leadership and Soviet armed forces, as well as large populations of civilians and ethnic groups, were purged of those deemed to be a threat or disloyal to Stalin. Millions were executed, put on trial, or sent to harsh prison camps known as *Gulags*. Many members left the party as they were shocked by the revelations and no longer wanted to be associated with it.

Until at least the 1960s, opposition to communism and international socialism – and to the politics of the Soviet Union – often had significant religious underpinnings, not least because church affiliation in Scotland remained higher than in England and grounded much of political culture. The Cold War had repercussions not only in discussions between the various denominations in Scotland but also within them.

Religious anti-communism in the Church of Scotland can be traced back to the end of the First World War, but it was revived in the context of the Cold War. What distinguished the anti-communism of the Kirk (the Church of Scotland) from that of churches elsewhere in the United Kingdom was its focus on highlighting its role as a moral authority through Christian action. Its evangelical 'Tell Scotland' campaign embedded a strong anti-communist message within a broader campaign of social transformation: the Kirk wanted to overcome the 'spiritual vacuum' of Scottish society because of a development that emphasised material goods rather than spiritual wellbeing.[31]

The Kirk's engagement with Cold War political culture went beyond anti-communism, however. The General Assembly of the Church of Scotland embarked on a research study called the 'Special Commission on Communism' in 1949. This culminated in three published reports: *The Challenge of Communism* (1951), *The Church Under Communism* (1953) and *The Church Faces the Challenge* (1955); and an unpublished internal report on church theology. Rather than demonise Marxism and lament communism's failings, the Commission endorsed a view of a progressive and modern Scottish society built on Christian tenets and perspectives. There was a diversity of voices in the Cold War debates.

Scottish Catholicism, widespread especially in the working class in the west of Scotland, also remained staunchly anti-communist, but mostly adopted the official reading propagated by the Pope. Here, as for example in the Catholic Workers' Guild, the fight against communism appeared less as a byproduct of a campaign to renew society, but as an end in itself.[32]

From the mid-1960s onwards, the Churches began to lose their importance as reference points for political debate in Scotland, and religion became less widespread as a basis for morality in general. From the 1970s, the most significant religious arguments were made specifically against the Cold War and nuclear weapons. While society as a whole became less religious – the historian Callum Brown has written about the 'death of Christian Britain' in the early 1960s – peace movements maintained a significant religious orientation.[33] The extent to which campaigns against nuclear weapons rested on Christian perceptions of morality is remarkable.

Anti-Cold Warriors

The Kirk was never a homogenous organisation. As well as exhibiting anti-communism, the debates about the role of the Kirk in Cold War society also had an impact on campaigns against Cold War mobilisations. Left-wing members of the Church of Scotland played a key part in linking religion to Cold War politics in Scotland more generally. This is especially apparent when considering the Campaign for Nuclear Disarmament (CND) in Scotland.

The particularities of the history of the CND in Scotland might appear to be quite distinct from elsewhere in Britain, given the presence of nuclear weapons in Scotland and the close connections with some sections of the Scottish nationalist movement. But despite strong links to Scottish nationalism, the Scottish CND was always part of the national campaign rather than a genuinely different organisation.

As in other parts of the United Kingdom, initial developments stemmed from concerns about the fallout from nuclear weapons testing, which in Scotland gave rise to the foundation of the Edinburgh Council for the Abolition of Nuclear Weapons Tests in 1957. The Council emphasised the harm radioactive strontium in milk would do, particularly to pregnant women and to children. Following the call by the journalist Kingsley Martin in the *New Statesman* in November 1957 to set up a campaign for the United Kingdom's unilateral nuclear disarmament, CND branches shot up across Scotland.

The campaign in Scotland, like the national CND, was grounded in the belief that Britain was still a global power that could lead by example: if the United Kingdom started with nuclear disarmament, others would follow. What distinguished the Scottish campaign from elsewhere, however, was its frequent connection to religious causes. In 1958, a report from Inverurie, Aberdeenshire, boasted that 'the Movement springs entirely from the Presbyterian Church at present'.[34]

One early CND activist was George MacLeod, Moderator of the Church of Scotland Assembly (1957–58). MacLeod had been an infantry officer with the Argyll and Sutherland Highlanders in the First World War and was awarded the Military Cross for bravery. In 1938, he founded the Iona Community, which brought together Christian activists to restore the derelict Abbey on the island.

MacLeod and other progressive Kirk members regarded peace activism as a form of 'the reconciliation ... at the heart of the Gospel'.[35] Roger Gray, an optician on the Isle of Skye, who founded the Skye branch of the CND with Flora Reid and transformed his shop into a peace centre, also had a background in the Kirk.[36]

But the CND in Scotland cannot be reduced entirely to its religious dimensions. It also acted as a space in which new cultural forms and norms could be explored. By fusing 'protest with jazz, folk song and festivity' the campaign contributed to 'fracturing the atmosphere of moral austerity that Presbyterianism had imposed on Scottish culture'.[37]

The roots of this revival of folk music and jazz lay in the early 1950s, when young people came into contact with this music from the United States by listening to armed forces radio. Venues such as the CND Late Club in Glasgow, and bands like the Glasgow Eskimoes whose song 'Ding Dong Dollar' became widely known, helped to spread protest culture beyond the actual protest movement.

Being part of the CND increasingly became a more general marker for political opposition. In 1962, the former miner and socialist activist Lawrence Daly wrote: 'When young Scots are politically enthusiastic today they are to be seen sporting "Ban-the-Bomb" badges or "Free Scotland" badges, or both at the same time.'[38]

The Scottish National Party (SNP) was still a very small organisation in the early 1960s and did not yet have any MPs in Westminster. Nonetheless, Scottish nationalism and the campaign against nuclear weapons soon came to be seen as closely linked, both by Scottish CND members and by Scottish society more broadly.

The CND and the nationalists alike pointed to the dangers of radiation from nuclear weapons on Scottish agriculture and the countryside. They also pointed out that stationing nuclear weapons in Scotland would single out the country as a target for the Soviet Union (see pages 55–56). And they portrayed the deployment of first American and then British submarines into Scottish waters as a bureaucratic imposition by a remote London Government that ignored the interests of the Scottish people. Ironically, the argument that painted the London Government as alien to the Scottish values of freedom and individualism was one that the Conservative and Liberal Parties had used in their 1950s election campaigns against the Labour Party, but without linking it to constitutional issues.

CND thistle badge

Designed by Gerald Holtom in 1958, the Campaign for Nuclear Disarmament (CND) logo is made up of the semaphore signals for 'N' and 'D'. It became an international symbol of peace, protest and defiance. The thistle overlaying Holtom's design represents Scotland.

Image © National Museums Scotland

Opposite: 'Protest & Survive' postcard by Peter Kennard

'Unofficial War Artist' Peter Kennard's photomontages provided the CND with stark and thought-provoking imagery to support its cause. This postcard from 1980 parodied the Government issued 'Protect and Survive' civil defence pamphlet.

© Peter Kennard / Photography by National Museums Scotland

Have you ever wished you were better informed?

This argument also had a Cold War context; it contrasted Scottish freedom with socialist or communist collectivism. The CND in Scotland in the early 1960s was one of the first political campaigns in which this originally conservative position was reversed to make a case for the devolution of power to Scotland or indeed Scottish independence.[39] It even resonated with some on the Labour left, including the young George Robertson when he was a schoolboy in Dunoon. Robertson was to become the UK's Secretary of State for Defence and NATO Secretary General (see page 35).

Although the Labour Party counted some strong supporters of unilateral nuclear disarmament among its members – and unilateralism was especially strong in the Scottish Labour Party – the SNP was the only party formally opposed to nuclear weapons in Scotland. Later SNP MPs such as Margo MacDonald, Isabel Lindsay and William (Billy) Wolfe had all been CND members. Wolfe, later MP for West Lothian and leader of the SNP from 1969 to 1979, helped to organise the Peace March Scotland in 1982. He claimed that the current SNP party symbol – representing the St Andrews Cross and a thistle – was inspired by the famous CND sign.[40]

The CND in Scotland recognised early on that the Cold War was as much about material production as ideas, blending the concept of community building and conscientious production that had characterised the work on Iona back in 1938 with Cold War concerns. In 1963, Tom McAlpine, a member of the Iona Community, helped to set up a 'Factories for Peace' campaign. With £6000 of donations, he founded Rowen Engineering in Glasgow, named after the nineteenth-century Quaker industrialist and social reformer Robert Owen. The purpose of the company was to highlight the importance of producing useful goods for society in a small company carried by the community of work – as opposed to the production of vast military machines in large factories.

When the CND lost public support across the United Kingdom over the course of the 1960s and 1970s – as tensions between the United States and Soviet Union subsided – the Scottish CND remained more active than other branches, and began to highlight the links between capitalism and the nuclear arms race. Such campaigns offered the mirror image of the expansion of defence studies in Scotland, mentioned above, which saw the installation of a defence studies institute at the University of Edinburgh headed by the historian John Erickson. In the 1970s, Zoë Fairbairns, a feminist activist at the University of St Andrews, inspired by similar campaigns in America, drew up a list of Scottish universities that received funding from the Ministry of Defence. She published the list in a pamphlet titled *Study War No More* (1975).[41]

In light of the pronounced crisis of manufacturing in Scotland in the 1970s, CND linked the loss of jobs in Scotland – in what it saw as *productive* civilian industries – to investment in the *unproductive* military, arguing that 'Jobs, not bombs' should be the guideline for politics.

Opposite: Scientists Against Nuclear Arms leaflet, *c.* **1980s**

A range of protest groups emerged during the 1980s, each highlighting their specific concerns about nuclear energy. Scientists Against Nuclear Arms (SANA) emphasised the impact of nuclear energy on the environment.

Image © National Museums Scotland

SCOTTISH SANA FACT-SHEET NO. 27

NUCLEAR WEAPONS: FOOD SUPPLIES AND THE RURAL ENVIRONMENT.

Prompt Effects on Farm Animals:

Background: This fact-sheet, prepared by scientists from published information, is one of a series which summarises the effects of nuclear weapons on food supplies and the rural environment. It deals with the prompt effects which can be expected from single or multiple nuclear explosions upon farm animals, whether out-of-doors or under cover. Other fact-sheets (listed at the end) describe the delayed and indirect effects on animals, and deal with farm and fruit crops, forestry and fisheries.

The Principal Causes of Prompt Effects: Nuclear weapons explosions affect living things directly through three forms of rapid release of energy:- by (a) blast, (b) heat and (c) nuclear radiation. In line with the assumptions of the British Government's civil defence exercise 'Square Leg', data are given here for 1 Megaton fission/fusion bombs. These liberate the equivalent of 1 million tons of TNT (0.91 Megatons), and are between 40 and 70 times more powerful than the Nagasaki and Hiroshima fission bombs. In this simulated nuclear attack on Scotland, it was presumed that 24 weapons, each of 1-5 Megatons, exploded at 19 sites, in the air, or near the surface of ground or water.

(A) Blast Injury to Farm Animals: Deaths and severe injuries to farm animals (and indeed to humans and wildlife) would result from:- (1) a sudden 'wave' of extra air pressure (above atmospheric pressure) lasting about 2-4 seconds, and particularly damaging to the lungs; (2) a violent wind, throwing animals against walls, etc.; (3) flying stones, broken glass, etc.

A single 1 Megaton explosion at the ground surface would form a crater 30 acres (12 ha.) in extent, and kill 50-100% of farm animals over 820 acres. What is termed a 'typical air burst' (an explosion at around 2800 feet) would extend the area to 1460 acres. Outside these central zones (which would be about 1-2 miles across), many farm animals would receive sub-lethal injuries from blast, even if they were under cover. For instance, the danger from flying glass fragments would extend up to 8 miles away from the crater.

(B) Heat Injury to Farm Animals: The intense explosion also liberates a pulse of light and heat which is for instance capable of blinding animals up to 50 miles away, if on a clear day their eyes happened to be focussed on this fireball.

50-100% of exposed farm animals would be killed by a 1 Megaton explosion over the following areas:

	moderately clear day	unusually clear day
surface explosion	43,200 acres	66,500 acres
air explosion	67,500 acres	103,800 acres

Animals under cover would be partially protected, but might be subject to burning or asphixiation through spontaneous ignition of dry combustible material such as wood, hay, etc. up to a distance of 5-10 miles from 'ground zero'. Outside these central zones, exposed animals over a larger area would be more or less severely burned.

In the late 1970s and early 1980s, the Scottish CND revived as a broader social movement against nuclear weapons and the nuclear arms race more generally. It began to engage more directly with the environmental consequences of the nuclear arms race, and often with campaigns against the civilian use of nuclear power, such as the Scottish Campaign to Resist the Atomic Menace or SCRAM.

The revival was prompted by debates about stationing a new generation of nuclear weapons – the Trident missiles – in Scotland, as well as the deployment of medium-range cruise missiles elsewhere in Britain. While in London the Government interpreted these moves as a response to an increasingly aggressive Soviet Union, CND members emphasised the risk of further escalation. They now showed the consequences of nuclear war on Scotland much more graphically and drastically.

Rather than concentrating narrowly on unilateral disarmament as it had in the late 1950s and early 1960s, the CND in Scotland now broadened its focus to become a movement for peace as a project of social transformation. An end of the nuclear arms race could only be achieved if social and political norms were transformed.

This meant that protests themselves became representations of the kind of society activists wished to create. Such a focus on peace went hand-in-hand with a more prominent role for women in the campaign, as well as in increasingly explicit arguments about the importance of female empowerment and a nuclear-free future for the next generation. Similarly, connections to the nascent gay and lesbian movement highlighted the importance of diversity and mutual recognition for Scottish society.

Non-violent direct action, such as sit-downs at military bases, was more conspicuous than it had been in the early 1960s, and protesters established a peace camp outside the naval base at Faslane where the UK nuclear deterrent was based. Activists hoped that the peace camp would embody the values of diversity and social justice.

Established in June 1982 by Scottish CND members, with the help of Strathclyde Regional Council – a Scottish 'nuclear free' council – the Faslane peace camp was one of a series in the United Kingdom, Europe and the United States. It is now said to be the longest-running peace camp in the world, with its activists dubbed 'everyday security practitioners'. These members sought to make their political campaign against nuclear weapons part of their daily life and routine, and thereby confront what they saw as the top-down imposition of security policies.[42] Such activism often involved challenging what they regarded as the specifically masculine order of the military, either through subverting it or mocking it.

The Faslane peace camp is only one example of how mobilisation for disarmament could be maintained in the absence of specific policy decisions or deployments. With the slow superpower bridge-building from the mid-1980s onwards, the focus of peace campaigning shifted towards highlighting the supposed dangers of nuclear weapons. Special campaigns emerged across Scotland that highlighted the environmental impact of the stationing of nuclear weapons locally.

They also pointed out the consequences of a nuclear war, focusing specifically on the acquisition of the new Trident system that had been agreed upon by the Government in the early 1980s (see page 44). Inspired by the British film *Threads* (1984), which imagined the horrific impact of a nuclear attack on the city of Sheffield in England, they developed similar scenarios for areas of Scotland.

Peace March Scotland stops in Stirling

To enliven the Peace March Scotland campaign in 1982, Kristin Barrett acquired a clown costume to pass out balloons to children. Her daughter, Lucy (right), was unsure of her mum's new outfit.

Image © National Museums Scotland

Objects had an important status in these campaigns. The CND's homemade banners and pamphlets from the late 1950s and 1960s highlight the importance of crafting for anti-nuclear activism. In the early 1980s, there was an explosion of creativity within the Scottish CND: activists made or repurposed everyday objects to 'exert counterpower' – normal items such as prams or plastic bottles became 'disobedient objects' that challenged mainstream politics and society.[43] There were, for example, homemade earrings in the shape of a CND symbol; and badges with witty slogans speaking to the protesters' identity.

Peace campaigner Kristin Barrett from Blairgowrie in Perthshire was especially creative. Barrett, who had studied education at Edinburgh before joining the University's CND group, repurposed her daughter's pram as a stall from which to distribute leaflets and CND badges. During the Peace March Scotland from Inverness to Edinburgh in 1982, Barrett used a fabric softener bottle filled with dry beans, given to her by a Church of Scotland minister, as a protest tool and rattle (see pages 76–77).

Many in Scottish CND in the 1980s regarded the nuclear arms race as a by-product of the materialism of consumer societies, materialism, they thought, that made society forgetful of the dangers posed by nuclear

Kristin Barrett

Kristin Barret has been a passionate campaigner for nuclear disarmament for over sixty years. Kristin first began campaigning while studying at university in Aberdeen, aged 17, in 1960.

In the early 1960s, she participated in marches on RAF Edzell and Aldermaston, and in 1982 took part in the Peace March Scotland. During the latter, she improvised a rattle bottle from a 'Comfort' fabric softener bottle. She filled it with dried beans and adorned it with anti-nuclear stickers to be noisily shaken to attract attention on the march. On one side of the rattle bottle is a sticker opposing Trident nuclear weapons, on the reverse is a CND logo sticker produced by the Scottish Campaign to Resist the Atomic Menace known as SCRAM.

This creativity was also evident when she used her daughter's pram to take supplies of CND stickers, badges, balloons and leaflets to campaign around areas of Perthshire and beyond. The pram stall made appearances at peace camps at Greenham Common and at Faslane. Kristin remarked, 'that buggy was a godsend, because I had to have it for her, but it was like a walking office so there'd be space underneath for all the leaflets'.

In the early 2000s, Kristin donated her large collection of anti-nuclear posters, pamphlets, badges, earrings, stickers and other ephemera to National Museums Scotland. Through the process of donating, Kristin reflected on her campaigning efforts, commenting, 'I'd forgotten how much work I'd put into CND!'

Above and right: Rattle bottle used on the Peace March Scotland, with 'A Pram Stall?' leaflet

Images © National Museums Scotland

Top, left: CND symbol earring

Images © National Museums Scotland

Top, right: CND badge

Images © National Museums Scotland

Above: Kristin Barrett, on the left of the picture, with her pram stall

Images © National Museums Scotland

77

weapons. Kristin Barrett's rattle bottle converted a product typical of consumer society into an object that Barrett used to protest against the excesses of consumer society.[44] The history of the Scottish anti-warriors had come full circle. By the end of the Cold War, activists who protested against nuclear weapons, had, through their opposition, also become part of Cold War mobilisations.

Scotland's place

Discussing Cold War mobilisations in Scotland highlights that it was not just 'a peripheral country, stuck out on the north-west fringes of Europe'. It emphasises Scotland's strategic position 'overlooking the vast expanses of the North-East Atlantic'.[45] Examining the Cold War in Scotland therefore means shifting our gaze away from the centre of decision-making in London and from a focus on central Europe towards the north.

Cold War mobilisations in Scotland were, however, never entirely about Scotland's strategic position. This chapter has considered the ways in which Scotland took part in the broader Cold War: the importance of Scotland in military mobilisation, in terms of both people and military sites; the role of Scottish industry; and the ways Scottish society engaged with the Cold War, in politics, in protest movements and in culture and society more broadly.

The Cold War was not simply imposed on Scotland and on Scots from the outside, by political decisions taken elsewhere, in London, in Europe, in the United States, or the Soviet Union. Scottish people actively participated in Cold War mobilisations, by endorsing the military confrontation, by ideologically supporting it, by protesting against it, but also by eventually treating it as normal. Throughout this period of mobilisation, Scottish people not only engaged with developments in their own society and in the United Kingdom, they also encountered the Cold War through their connections around the world, as will be seen in the next chapter.

Notes

1. Fraser MacDonald, 'Geopolitics and "the vision thing": regarding Britain and America's first nuclear missile', *Transactions of the Institute of British Geographers* 31 (2006), p. 53.
2. John Davies and Alexander J. Kent, *The Red Atlas: How the Soviet Union Secretly Mapped the World* (Chicago: University of Chicago Press, 2017).
3. Malcolm Spaven, *Fortress Scotland: A Guide to the Military Presence* (London: Pluto Press, 1983).
4. Brian Lavery, *Shield of Empire: The Royal Navy and Scotland* (Edinburgh: Birlinn: 2007).
5. Niall Barr, 'The Cold War and Beyond', in Edward M. Spiers, Jeremy A. Crang and Matthew J. Strickland (eds), *A Military History of Scotland* (Edinburgh: Edinburgh University Press, 2012), pp. 600–24.
6. 'How Scotland and three CalMac ferries played a crucial part in nuclear planning', *The Herald*, 22 January 2017.
7. Spaven, *Fortress Scotland*, p. 2.
8. Trevor Royle, *Facing the Bear: Scotland and the Cold War* (Edinburgh: Birlinn, 2019).
9. Alison Campsie, 'The Scottish islands used as testing grounds', *The Scotsman*, 1 October 2020.
10. David Edgerton, *Warfare State: Britain, 1920–1970* (Cambridge: Cambridge University Press, 2006).
11. Robert Bud and Philip Gummett (eds), *Cold War, Hot Science: Applied Research in Britain's Defence Laboratories, 1945–1990* (Amsterdam: Harwood Academic/Science Museum, 1999), p. 25.
12. Alex Law, 'Melting the Cold War Permafrost in Scotland: Restructuring Military Industry in Scotland', *Antipode* 31 (1999), pp. 421–52.
13. Spaven, *Fortress Scotland*.
14. Cited in Law, 'Cold War Permafrost', p. 431.
15. Law, 'Cold War Permafrost', p. 431.
16. Royle, *Facing the Bear*.
17. John Lovering and Martin Boddy, 'The Geography of Military Industry in Britain', *Area* 20 (1988), pp. 41–51.
18. John Lovering, 'The Changing Geography of the Military Industry in Britain', *Regional Studies* 25 (1991), pp. 279–93.
19. Sarah A. Harper, 'Bombers, Bunkers, and Badges. The Cold War Materialised in National Museums Scotland', unpublished PhD thesis, University of Stirling, 2022.
20. Richard Vinen, *National Service. Conscription in Britain 1945–1963* (London: Allen Lane, 2014), p. 399.
21. Cited in Vinen, *National Service*, p. 113.
22. Vinen, *National Service*, pp. 156–57.
23. Vinen, *National Service*, p. 207.
24. Richard Finlay, 'National Identity, Union, and Empire, c. 1850–c. 1970', in John MacKenzie and T. M. Devine (eds), *Scotland and the British Empire* (Oxford: Oxford University Press, 2011), pp. 280–316, p. 311.
25. This was the title of a 2007 BBC documentary on the fortieth anniversary of the Aden campaign. For context see Richard Finlay, 'National Identity', in Mackenziee and Devine (eds), *Scotland and the British Empire*, pp. 314–15.
26. David French, *Military Identities. The Regimental System, the British Army, & the British People, c. 1870–2000* (Oxford: Oxford University Press, 2005), p. 243.
27. Stuart Allan, 'Beating retreat: The Scottish military tradition in decline', in Bryan S. Glass and John M. MacKenzie (eds), *Scotland, Empire and Decolonisation in the Twentieth Century* (Manchester: Manchester University Press, 2017), pp. 131–54.
28. David French, *Military Identities*.
29. W. W. Knox, *Industrial Nation. Work, Culture and Society in Scotland, 1800–Present* (Edinburgh: Edinburgh University Press, 1999), p. 301.
30. Willie Thompson, 'Scottish Communists during the Cold War', in Brian P. Jamieson (ed.), *Scotland and the Cold War* (Dunfermline: Cualann Press, 2003), pp. 39–69.
31. Elaine W. McFarland and Ryan G. Johnston, 'The Church of Scotland's Special Commission on Communism, 1949–1954: Tackling "Christianity's Most Serious Competitor"', *Contemporary British History* 23 (2009), pp. 337–61, p. 347.
32. McFarland and Johnston, 'The Church of Scotland's Special Commission on Communism'.
33. Callum G. Brown, *The Death of Christian Britain: Understanding Secularisation 1800–2000*, 2nd edn (London: Routledge, 2009).
34. Quoted in Christopher R. Hill, 'Nations of Peace: Nuclear Disarmament and the Making of National Identity in Scotland and Wales', *Twentieth Century British History* 27 (2016), pp. 26–50, p. 35.
35. Quoted in Alastair Ramage, 'The Role of the Churches in the Peace Movement', in Jamieson (ed.), *Scotland and the Cold War*, pp. 31–38, p. 31. From Iona Community's Justice and Peace Commitment.
36. Royle, *Facing the Bear*.
37. Angela Bartie, *The Edinburgh Festivals: Culture and Society in Post-war Britain* (Edinburgh: Edinburgh University Press, 2013), pp. 91, 229.
38. Quoted in Hill, 'Nations of Peace', p. 49.
39. Malcolm Petrie, *Politics and the People: Scotland, 1945–1979* (Edinburgh: Edinburgh University Press, 2022).
40. Hill, 'Nations of Peace'.
41. Zoë Fairbairns, *Study War No More: Military Involvement in British Universities and Colleges* (London: The Campaign, 1974).
42. Catherine Eschle, 'Nuclear (in)security in the everyday: Peace campers as everyday security practitioners', *Security Dialogue* 49 (2018), pp. 289–305.
43. Catherine Flood and Gavin Grindon (eds), *Disobedient Objects* (London: V&A Publishing, 2014).
44. Harper, 'Bombers, Bunkers, and Badges'.
45. Spaven, *Fortress Scotland*, p. 1.

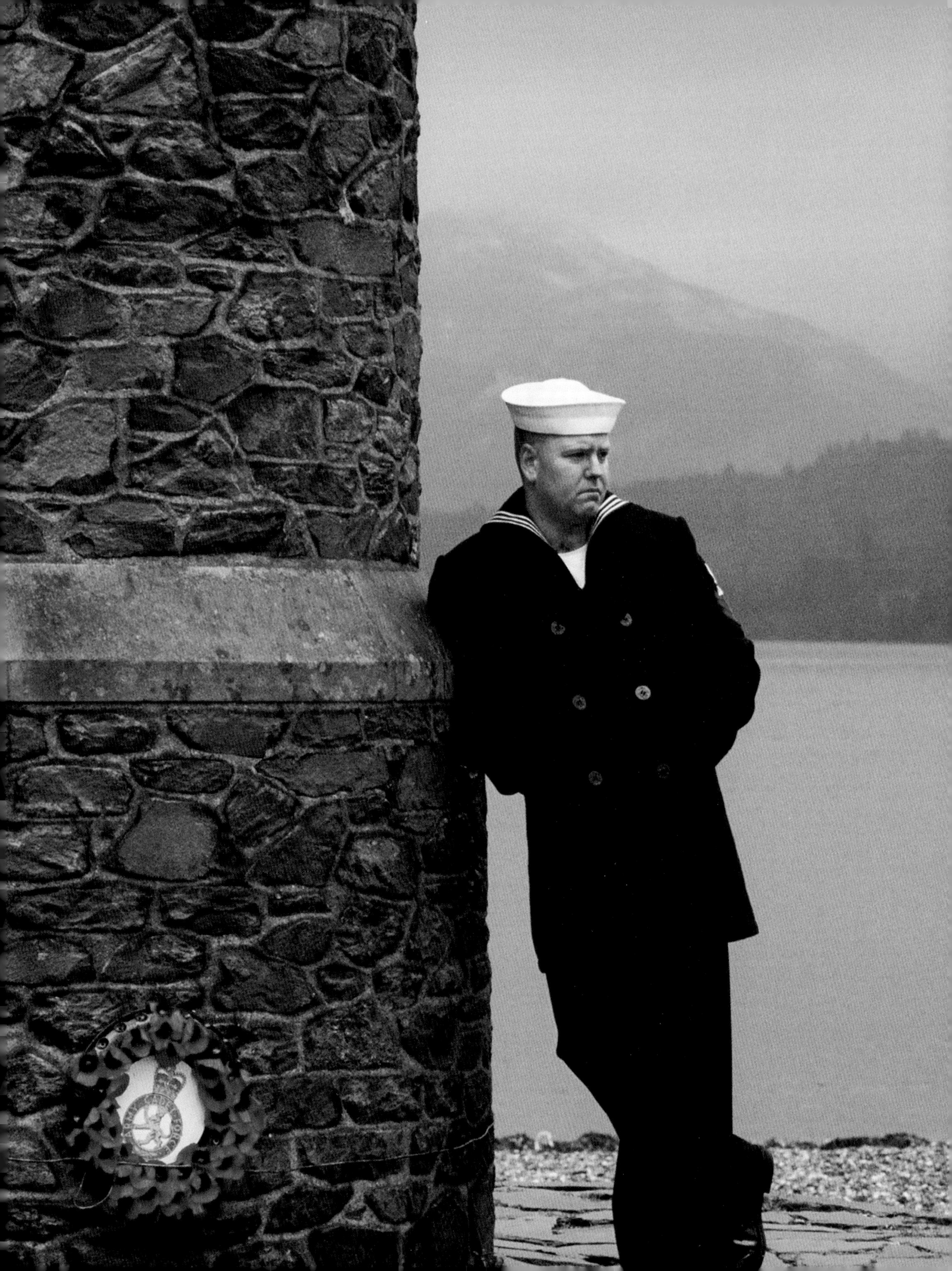

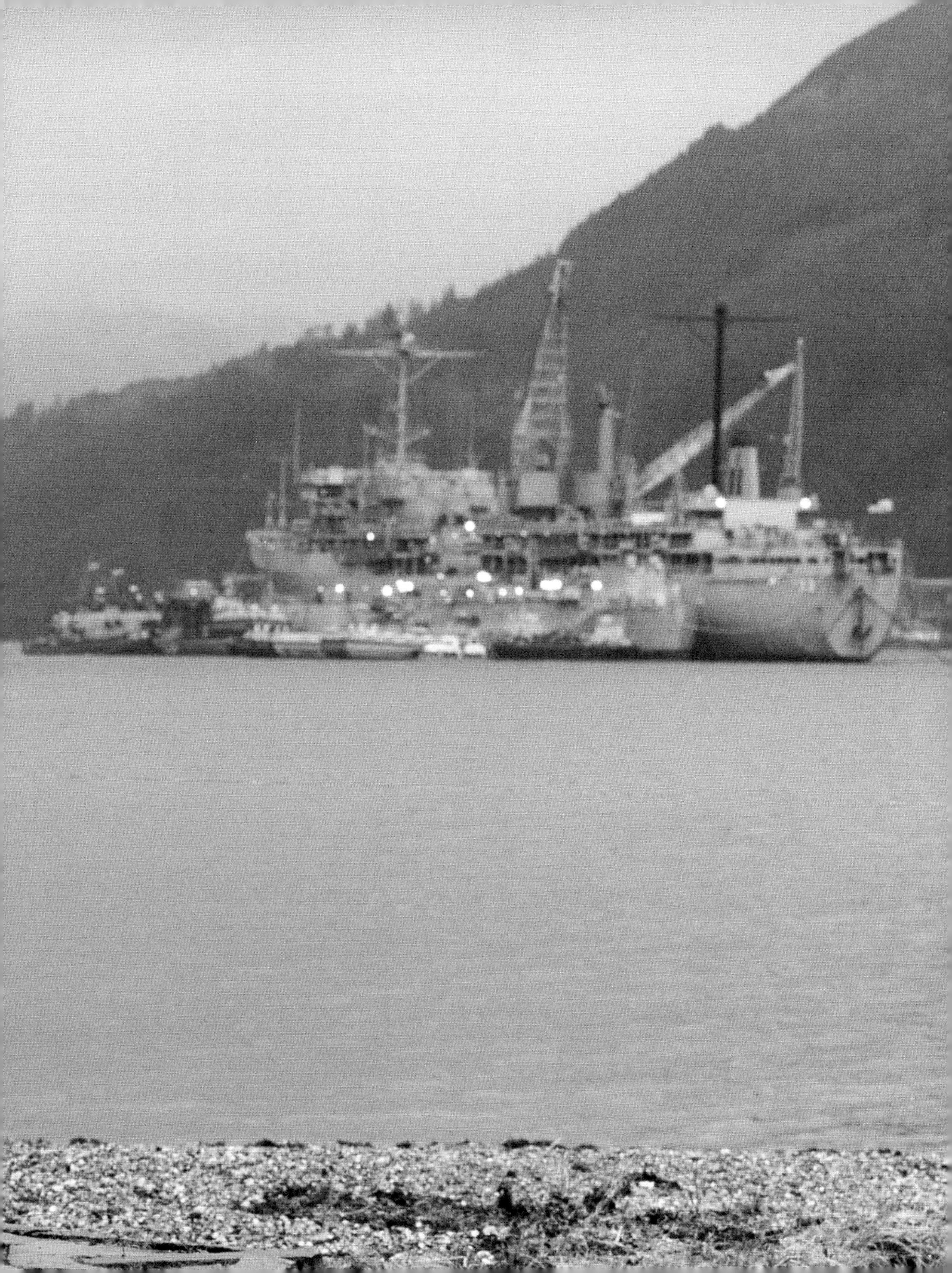

Chapter 3

Cold War connections

In 1951, a delegation of trade unionists from Scotland visited Ukraine. at that time part of the Soviet Union. They came back with positive impressions and saw their visit and the hospitality of their hosts as a way to establish peace during the Cold War:

> Peace, in our opinion, is the one thing upon which all people, irrespective of race, colour, or religion are united. Let us then accept the hand of friendship so freely offered to us by the Soviet people, ensure world peace and an opportunity for all peoples to achieve their own destinies and win for themselves a better life.[1]

The Cold War tends to be remembered as an era of deep-seated animosity and secrecy that divided societies in Eastern and Western Europe by geography, politics and ideology. However, despite walls, weapons and words separating East and West, the example of this delegation in Ukraine shows that there were connections across the Cold War divide. Cold War Scotland was part of these connections in many different ways, from tourism to creative endeavour, scholarly diplomacy to sporting events.

These connections were not, however, as straightforward as the impressions of the Scottish trade unionists suggest. While they stressed the peacefulness of the Soviet Union and the liberation of its workers, the Soviet Union waged a proxy war in Korea and oppressed its population at home. Connections across the Iron Curtain were dynamic and sometimes strained, as were relationships between countries and within societies on both sides of it.

Such tensions will be explored within this chapter, via a number of issues and on different levels, including organisations such as the Scottish communists and socialists. In seeking to establish connections to the Soviet Union, these groups were often branded as outsiders who worked with 'the enemy'. We will also meet individuals, such as singer Paul Robeson, poet Hugh MacDiarmid, tourist Eileen Crawford and university professor John Erickson, and visit specific locations in Scotland, including Dunoon and Ullapool.

Pages 80–81: End of the American era

Petty officer David Bernett contemplates life away from Scotland as the support ship USS *Simon Lake* prepares for the US Navy's departure from the Holy Loch in 1992.

© *Herald & Evening Times* (Newsquest). Licensor www.SCRAN.ac.uk

Opposite: Communist graffiti on Edinburgh Castle

The Communist Party of Great Britain was especially popular in Scotland. Here, communist slogans are cleaned from the walls of Edinburgh Castle.

© The Scotsman Publications. Licensor www.SCRAN.ac.uk

As outlined in previous chapters, the Cold War was a political, economic and military phenomenon for Scots – now its presence in culture and social life will be discussed.

Cold War culture

The most immediate connections Scots forged with the Cold War outside the United Kingdom and Europe were based on ideological affinities. Other countries were places in which an individual's hopes for the future could be projected. This can be seen, for example, in attempts to establish common ideological links across the Atlantic through organisations such as the Congress for Cultural Freedom (CCF), an international organisation which aimed to bring together like-minded academics and intellectuals who opposed communism.

For some countries, for example Finland, associations like the Scottish-Finnish Society became part of its formal foreign policy. Finland remained neutral in the Cold War rather than part of any military alliance, keeping most of its social connections with the Soviet Union due to its geographical proximity. The Scottish-Finnish Society offered one way to broaden this outlook.[2]

The connections that socialists and communists in Scotland forged with the Soviet Union and Eastern Europe might be the most revealing in terms of their inherent contradictions. In Scotland, as elsewhere, ideologies were bundled up with moral assumptions. These influenced how people responded to a perceived 'enemy' in their politics and everyday lives. To some groups, the Iron Curtain was a divide to be crossed and undermined; to others it was one to be reinforced. Such positions often rested on existing attitudes towards communism, capitalism and cultural understandings of the Soviet Union, China and the United States that preceded the period of the Cold War.

Miners, for example, had a long tradition of radical left-wing politics.[3] While this did not necessarily mean that Scottish miners were communists, the miners' association with the industrial struggles of the international working classes significantly diminished their acceptance of Cold War superpower politics after 1945. In the post-war period, the National Union of Miners Scottish Area (NUMSA) actively promoted Scottish interests not only through organised labour, but within the arts and culture too.

These activities separated Scottish mining from the National Coal Board (NCB), the body created by the British Government to run the mines when they were in national ownership until the 1980s. The NUMSA framed its members' activities in the context of the international workers' movement. Its leadership was affiliated to the Communist Party of Great Britain (CPGB) in this period, and while the CPGB did not dictate the views of Scottish miners, their steer influenced the union's activities and annual programme.[4]

Miners at the National Union of Miners HQ, Edinburgh

There was considerable support for communism among Scottish industrial and mining communities. The Communist Party of Great Britain had some support from the Scottish Trades Union Congress. This image shows miners gathering for an anti-communist demonstration outside the National Union of Miners headquarters in Edinburgh in 1956.

© The Scotsman Publications. Licensor www.SCRAN.ac.uk

Paul Robeson in Scotland

In 1949, Paul Robeson, the singer and civil rights activist, visited Scotland in association with the National Union of Miners Scottish Area. Due to Robeson's socialist views and his visits to the Soviet Union, the US Government issued a travel ban in the 1950s.

© The Scotsman Publications. Licensor www.SCRAN.ac.uk

In 1949, as part of its cultural remit, the NUMSA organised a concert featuring the popular African-American singer Paul Robeson at the Usher Hall in Edinburgh. Robeson's biography and his connections with Scotland highlight how the traditional view of the Cold War as a contest between two blocs does not do justice to experiences of the Cold War in Scotland. The example of Robeson shows the multiple connections between developments in the United States and in Scotland, and demonstrates how campaigns for socialism and communism were not merely a part of societies in Eastern Europe, but formed an important avenue of political engagement in Scotland and the West more generally.

Robeson first visited Britain in the 1920s as a stage performer.[5] During repeated tours of the country he deepened his political convictions based on the collective concerns of oppressed people. While his American upbringing led him to focus his activism on Black civil rights, he was also moved by the situation of working-class people worldwide. Robeson's name soon stood for the politics of the class struggle, and he actively supported workers' groups, such as miners from South Wales, in their campaigns for better employment conditions.

The NUMSA's event in 1949, attended by miners from all over Scotland, was preceded by a recital arranged by the NCB at Woolmet Colliery in Midlothian. Footage of the event shows Robeson eating a meal in the miners' canteen and taking a tour of the coalface.[6] The highlight came when he sang 'Joe Hill' to an audience of miners, a song that emphasised working-class organisation and the power of justice to prevail in the long term.[7]

Paul Robeson soon became a star within industrial communities across Britain. But as anti-communism became more firmly embedded in political culture from the early 1950s onwards, he became the subject of intense scrutiny by the US Government and the House Committee of Un-American

Activities. In 1950, his politics were deemed dangerously radical and his passport was revoked on the grounds that he was a communist sympathiser.[8]

Scottish workers supported Robeson's case for freedom of movement. This was demonstrated in 1951, when he was nominated by students at the University of Aberdeen for the post of 'Scottish Lord Rectorship'. From 1954, the Scottish Trades Union Congress campaigned for the return of his passport; and Scottish MPs and actors petitioned President Eisenhower on Robeson's behalf.

Following the restoration of his passport and travel rights in 1958, Robeson recommenced his work in the United Kingdom and gave frequent interviews to the British press, including one in which he remarked, 'I'm very pro-Scottish' with 'loads' of friends in Scotland.[9] In 1960, he was an honorary guest at the Glasgow May Day Parade.[10]

While some miners were sympathetic towards communism, there were many who did not support Stalinist ideology, and others who were anti-communist. In defending Robeson's right to American citizenship and free movement, however, they joined the international effort to unite oppressed groups across Cold War divides.

Robeson loved languages and this brought him to the attention of the Scottish arts scene. The connections he drew between world languages reflected his conviction that a universal cultural spirit was at the heart of equality. His activism became part of the ways in which he constructed an image of himself as a global citizen who was at the same time familiar with local traditions.

From the 1960s, Robeson's self-image resonated with attempts in Scotland to return to authentic Scottish folk music, tales, traditions and language as a journey of rediscovery of democratic traditions. These were believed to have been lost not only with the onset of manufacturing modernity during the Industrial Revolution, but especially with the arrival of what many activists regarded as the conformist culture of the Cold War. By engaging with Robeson, many Scots were prompted to engage with their own traditions.

Robeson had started to learn Gaelic in 1938, and on several occasions he sang Hebridean songs, with his travels around Scotland taking him to local sites of traditional folk music.[11] His attention to Gaelic earned him the respect of many Scots, including literary figures such as Hugh MacDiarmid (the pen name of Christopher Murray Grieve), one of the poets who had led the Scottish literary renaissance during the 1920s and 1930s.

In 1968, on Robeson's seventieth birthday, MacDiarmid contributed to a programme of events in celebration of the singer and activist. In his honour, the Scottish actor and producer, Alex McCrindle, read a stanza of MacDiarmid's poem 'Third Hymn to Lenin, the Soviet Revolutionary':

… thou fire of freedom,
Fire-like in your purity and heaven-seeking vehemence,
Yet the adjective must not suggest merely meteoric,
Spectacular—not the flying sparks but the intense
Glowing core of your character, your large and splendid stability,
Made you the man you are—a live heart of all humanity![12]

After transitioning to communist politics in the 1930s, MacDiarmid's poetry praised the Soviet Union and its leaders – past and present.[13] Nonetheless, his position did not easily fit into party politics, and in the 1930s he was expelled from the CPGB for being too nationalist, as the CPGB had changed its course from emphasising nationalism to emphasising internationalism. He was also expelled from the Scottish National Party for being too communist.[14] A divisive figure, MacDiarmid held a range of views – for example about women and same-sex couples – that we do not find palatable today.

When the crimes committed by the Soviet dictator Joseph Stalin during the 1930s became public knowledge, support for communism dwindled in the West. Even the Soviet Union had distanced itself from Stalin. MacDiarmid, however, maintained an immovable vision of Soviet communism for the rest of his life, even when it was no longer fashionable.

In 1957, when MacDiarmid wrote a piece in the communist publication *Daily Worker* in which he associated the National Paul Robeson Committee with communism, the Committee was quick to respond, asking him to rectify the false association. They feared that MacDiarmid's statement would serve as an additional justification for the United States Government's withdrawal of Robeson's travel rights.[15]

Many at the time disapproved of folk music and folk poetry. To these critics, folk music and a specifically Scottish perspective were linked to a socialist or communist milieu and hindered rather than enhanced international connections. This can be seen by considering the debates about the Edinburgh festivals that were initially launched in 1947.

The festivals were clearly Christian in origin, with art and music serving as a 'bond of union in a disintegrated world' that allowed everyone to 'breathe together a tranquil atmosphere of spiritual unity'. Sir Andrew Murray, Edinburgh's Provost and, at the time, the chair of the Edinburgh International Festival, saw the event in 1949 as a way to resolve conflicts. Culture thereby became a 'moral and intellectual guiding force in the future of the world' that would help create 'a lofty spirit of freedom'.[16]

Not everyone agreed with this assessment, however, and MacDiarmid was particularly outspoken in his criticism. In a column in *The Scotsman*, he argued that the Edinburgh International Festival was, like the city that hosted it, a 'stronghold of bourgeois decadence'. He, like others, failed to acknowledge the Scottish elements of the culture on offer.[17]

This debate over what counted as 'culture' in Cold War Scotland was the beginning of the Edinburgh Festival Fringe; some theatre groups turned up without an invitation and offered drama and marionette theatre during, but not as part of, the Festival. From the early 1950s, these performances on the fringe attracted almost more media attention than the actual event.

Communist newspapers such as *Daily Worker* called the Fringe the 'People's Festival' that appealed to the 'ordinary man' and was 'hitting the target'.[18] Soon it became a symbol of what contemporaries saw as a new cultural offer that appealed especially to young people. Critics saw this as very dangerous for the cohesion of Scottish society in trying to fight against communism.

Some in the Church of Scotland, which had played an important role in framing the main Festival, were alarmed: a Reverend Robertson, for example, saw only 'drunkenness, sordidness and immorality'. Edinburgh's Fringe thus became a focus of international Christian lobbying. The American Moral Rearmament Group conducted missions on 'an ideological whirlwind'

Yevgeny Yevtushenko

Yevgeny Yevtushenko reading 'Three Hymns to Lenin' by Hugh MacDiarmid. Although the two poets held conflicting views on socialism, MacDiarmid welcomed Yevtushenko warmly to Scotland, and the poets exchanged tokens of friendship.

University of Dundee. The Peto Collection.

to impress upon young people the importance of living 'in a reorganised world under the guidance of God' rather than a godless communist dictatorship.[19]

Connecting ideologies

Cultural activities in the 1950s and 60s both contributed to and bypassed the supposed confrontation between communism on the one hand and liberal democracy and capitalism on the other. As in the context of the Edinburgh Festivals, it is also observable in the ways in which poets like Hugh MacDiarmid engaged with these orthodoxies.

In 1962, MacDiarmid hosted the Soviet poet Yevgeny Yevtushenko at his cottage in Biggar, South Lanarkshire.[20] MacDiarmid was seen as one of the greatest Scottish poets, and there was significant interest among contemporary Soviet writers and poets in Scottish folk traditions, both as expressions of authentic life and sources for social change.

Unlike MacDiarmid, Yevtushenko took a critical position on Stalinism, and the two poets debated their ideological differences. MacDiarmid offered Yevtushenko a copy of his book *Three Hymns to Lenin*. The encounter demonstrated that connections did not always go hand-in-hand with agreement, but showed how the two poets represented two versions of socialist politics and two competing visions of the future.

MacDiarmid's travels as a cultural ambassador did not shift his communist orthodoxy either. In 1950 he visited the Soviet Union, and in 1957 the People's Republic of China – but neither occasion gave him cause to question his party loyalty. In 1964, MacDiarmid ran as a CPGB candidate for the local parliamentary election in the Kinross and West Perthshire constituency under his original name Christopher M. Grieve. In his campaign pamphlet he argued that he stood for the 'right of the Scottish people to control their own affairs', elaborating:

> The Communist Party is the only party which deals realistically with Scottish industry and employment. It is the only Party which gives education priority, which supports the new Socialist governments of Cuba, Algeria and North Vietnam and the national independence of the new African states. Which refuses to allow the national wealth to be squandered on gigantic and useless 'defence' schemes.[21]

MacDiarmid's poetry and politics linked Scottish nationalism with his strident internationalism.

However, the way MacDiarmid channelled his internationalism through his allegiance to the CPGB seemed increasingly out of place by the early 1960s. The writer Alexander Trocchi, who was born in Glasgow and attended the University of Glasgow before moving to Paris and the United States, offered a different version of cultural internationalism.

Trocchi had become a major voice of avant-garde or experimental culture in the 1950s. He was part of what became known as the Situationist International, a left-wing cultural movement that sought to move beyond the restrictions of Cold War culture by staging controversial events and by practising new lifestyles.

Yevgeny Yevtushenko and Hugh MacDiarmid

Russian poet Yevgeny Yevtushenko presents Hugh MacDiarmid with a Russian doll and bottle of vodka outside MacDiarmid's Brownsbank cottage, Biggar, in 1962.

University of Dundee. The Peto Collection.

While living in New York in the 1950s, he had poked fun at the dominant norms by carrying a wooden pulpit around with him when out to buy drugs; when the police were close, he put the pulpit down and started preaching in order to avoid arrest.

Trocchi met MacDiarmid at the Scottish International Writers' Conference held in Edinburgh in 1962. During a discussion about nationalism and Scottish culture, he called MacDiarmid an 'old fossil' and the literature he represented 'turgid, petty, provincial, the stale-porridge, Bible-clasping nonsense'. Rather than focusing on nationalism, Trocchi argued, literature should focus on questions of human identity. And rather than focusing on high politics as a means of change, he advocated for personal transformation and self-discovery as the only route towards a meaningful life.[22]

MacDiarmid, in turn, represented Trocchi as an unthinking follower of American trends, when the country had 'gone absolutely rotten in the bulk of its production', which had led him, quite contrary to what we think is acceptable today, to see 'lesbianism, homosexuality and matters of that kind' as the 'burning questions in the world today'.[23]

Elsewhere, connections with the Soviet Union were based on the experiences of the Second World War. The Scotland-USSR Society, for example, was founded by Scottish intellectuals in 1945 as an attempt to connect their own country and the Soviet Union. During the war, the Soviet Union became an important ally for Britain in the fight against German National Socialism and Japanese imperialism. The Society was intended to be a means to keep this anti-fascism alive in the post-war period and was one of a number of such organisations founded across the United Kingdom.

From the early 1950s, however, the Scotland-USSR Society became as much an instrument of Soviet cultural diplomacy as of grassroots desires for mutual understanding. John Kinloch, opening the Society's headquarters in Friendship House in Glasgow as its President, gave expression to both: 'There are three alternatives before the world: annihilation, peaceful co-existence based on a fear of the Bomber, or friendship … . This house is going to be a centre dedicated to building up peace between nations.'[24]

The Society served as an intermediary for organising tours to the Soviet Union and, from 1961, supported the travel company Sovscot Tours Limited, which sought to offer package tours to the Soviet Union and thus capitalise on the growth of mass tourism.

Such connections served not only as markers of international solidarity, but also as signs of Cold War fears and subversion. Whereas for participants in the Scottish-USSR Society, the Soviet Union was a place of innovative social change, the American Central Intelligence Agency (CIA) regarded such initiatives as only thinly veiled attempts by the Soviet Union to undermine Western unity in the Cold War, and feared that the USSR would exploit such societies 'to the greatest extent possible'.[25]

Often, friendship societies were the subject of fierce internal debates that played out the ideological battles of the Cold War on a small scale. Poles who had settled in Scotland before the Cold War – for example, working in the mining industry – had their own community organisations that sought to promote Polish culture within Scotland.

There was no consensus among these groups, however, as to how to interpret the arrival of a communist dictatorship in their mother country. A report from 1958 concluded:

Left: *Chairman Mao Goes to Anyuan*, Jiangxi Silk Factory, c.1968

Some items in National Museum Scotland's collections speak to the ways in which the Chinese 'cultural revolution' was represented at home and abroad. For example, this silk artwork, *Chairman Mao Goes to Anyuan*, is from around 1968.

Image © National Museums Scotland

Right: *Celebrating the Harvest* porcelain figurine, Jingdezhen, c.1970

This porcelain figurine *Celebrating the Harvest* from Jingdezhen in the 1970s depicts 14 figures celebrating around a large wheatsheaf with the Chinese character feng (abundance). This scene is based on an opera about the heroism of communists during the Chinese Cultural Revolution.

Image © National Museums Scotland

At present there is a crisis affecting the Poles in exile. The émigré masses have become alienated and disillusioned. Many have stopped participating in community activities. Fighting among themselves, the Polish political parties and leaders in exile have lost their authority and support.[26]

Indeed, Scotland had aroused the special interest of the Soviet Union and other Eastern European countries as a target for propaganda campaigns. Scottish nationalism seemed to offer a way in which to destabilise the United Kingdom and also, in its left-wing versions, seemed to align well with the ideological emphasis on local folklore and folk traditions in the Soviet Union from the 1970s or so. The presence of US military installations in Scotland and the opposition among some Scots against this, offered a political inroad into Scottish society. Such connections could be disruptive. For example, in 2003 Helen Sanderson from Arbroath, in Angus, admitted that she had been a spy for the Stasi, the East German spy service, during the 1980s while a member of the CND.[27]

In the 1960s, China became a more important reference for the Scottish left. From the early part of that decade, China increasingly presented itself as an alternative to the socialism of the Soviet Union. This attracted some who had been unhappy about the emphasis on state direction in the Soviet Union and wanted to see more direct social involvement in planning a socialist revolution. Chinese leader Mao Zedong's 'cultural revolution' during that time was a gigantic exercise in social mobilisation that led to millions of deaths of those who did not comply. Nonetheless, some left-wing activists found the emphasis on youth involvement attractive and adopted Maoism as part of their own participation in student activism.

By the early 1960s, then, different versions of how to connect Scotland to the world in the context of the Cold War had developed. And there was less and less agreement among Scots on what these connections meant.

Visitors from afar

If some Scots encountered their global peers through organisations with ideological motives, for others Cold War connections were part of everyday life in their local communities. This was particularly the case for those in rural or semi-rural areas who engaged with the American sailors who arrived as part of the deployment of nuclear submarines to the Holy Loch in the early 1960s (see page 34). The area around its main town of Dunoon was largely rural and depended on agriculture and tourism during the summer months. The base and the people that lived in it brought a major social transformation.

A large notice at the gangway of the American depot ship read: 'You are about to represent your country in Scotland. Do so with pride, dignity and honour.' Even so, connections between the base personnel and locals were complex. The town of Dunoon had around 9000 residents: the arrival of more than 3000 US Navy personnel and their families, on the base and ashore, increased the population by a third.

Small businesses profited – especially the local taxi trade; for a spell, Dunoon had the highest proportion of taxi drivers of any town in Europe. Adverts even appeared in the local press in 1961 offering Glasgow taxis for sale.

However, newspapers also reported that it was increasingly hard for local businesses to find women available to work after 5.30pm, because they wanted to go out with the American sailors. Americans had a reputation for being wealthy, and there were rumours that they took women to the dance halls in Glasgow. In 1963, an enterprising local resident set up a new club on Argyle Street in Dunoon. The Monaco Club catered to US Navy personnel in particular and was modelled on Las Vegas casinos.[28]

Rather than saviours from the Soviet threat, some saw American sailors as dangerous predators out to seduce local women. Venereal diseases and illegitimate children were of particular concern. The *Glasgow Evening Times* observed in January 1962:

> Since the arrival of the American sailors at Dunoon it is only out of politeness that the community has suffered in silence the embarrassment caused by some American sailors keeping their secret passion anything but secret. Any Scottish girl and boy behaving as these sailors do would be thrown out of railway stations and other public places by the scruff of their necks.[29]

Dunoon shopkeepers hoping to benefit from prosperous American sailors were disappointed when these potential customers mostly bought their everyday provisions from stores on the base. The local press featured complaints by traders who argued that the Americans had been ungrateful.

One correspondent in March 1963 probably spoke for many when arguing that the distribution of wealth and opportunity between the settled population and the newcomers was unfair, mostly because hosting the American submarine base meant becoming a likely target for Soviet attacks:

> American goods are available at dirt-cheap prices to our country's detriment as they pay no import duty or purchase tax. But, now to beat it all we are going to build them bowling alleys and recreation rooms. If we are going to share the dangers (as a frontline town), then let us merit the same facilities that they enjoy.[30]

The arrival of so many new people in Dunoon and the Cowal peninsula also put pressure on the housing market. Americans and their families benefitted from financial support beyond their salaries for paying rent, leading to a significant increase in local rents. This had a particular impact on young families. Building more houses was not an easy solution because the topography – a small coastal strip with rising hills behind – was challenging.

Schools in the area were also adversely affected in catering for the children of American personnel as well as the local population. And when authority rates rose significantly in 1967, many residents blamed the Americans.[31] A letter to the local newspaper expressed dismay about 'playing Santa Claus to the Americans all the year round'.[32]

But locals also have many positive memories of the Americans in and around Dunoon. Their arrival prompted new infrastructure and entertainment facilities that might otherwise have taken longer to come to the relatively secluded community. And despite the concerns voiced above, some local women did marry American sailors. Dunoon native Andrene Messersmith, fondly recalls:

> … what a generous people Americans are. Their casual hospitality … introduced us to their plentiful cheap liquor in the form of Southern Comfort, Jack Daniels and Harvey Wallbangers …. We ate their pasta, pizzas, pretzels, their hot dogs and hamburgers. Betty Crocker cake mixes and muffin mixes offered us the lazy way to bake.[33]

For many, the American presence became a sign of growing affluence. Tom Reid, a schoolboy in the early 1960s, remembered how an American sailor gave 'us three ragamuffins a lift in his huge Yankee car', and how big the barbecues were at the parties organised by the base to engage the locals: 'Mountains of Coke and barrels of ice, salad and desserts aplenty.' Barbecues and hamburgers were new to many.[34]

The American presence gradually became a marker of the town's modernity. When the US base was dissolved after the end of the Cold War in 1991, locals felt a sense of nostalgia and were concerned by the withdrawal of a source of economic opportunities.

Elsewhere on the Scottish coast, social connections extended east rather than west. The small port village of Ullapool, on the north-west coast, was the unlikely setting for Cold War encounters. From the 1970s, an increasing number of factory ships from Poland, Bulgaria, East Germany and the Soviet Union sailed to Scottish waters to catch and process herring, and later mackerel. Such fish were very popular in continental Europe as a cheap source of nutrients – and cash-strapped Eastern European countries sold them for valuable Western currency.

At the same time, fishing vessels offered the Soviet Union an inconspicuous way of spying on British and American defence installations in Scotland – although not secret enough to avoid suspicion among the intelligence services and the British Ministry of Defence. While an official at the Ministry noted that having processing ships out at sea was preferable to having them in ports, he was still concerned about the 'potential for intelligence gathering against us'.[35]

Because of a Government-imposed ban on foreign trawlers fishing in British coastal waters, overseas traders looked to Scottish and Irish fishermen to supply their catches, which would in turn be processed and frozen onboard factory ships known as 'Klondykers'. Referencing the gold rushes in America, the term 'klondyking' was probably coined by the fishing industry in the late nineteenth century. It referred to local fishermen immediately selling their catch (here primarily herring) to processing ships to be preserved for transport.[36]

Ships from all over the world became permanent fixtures on Loch Broom (Ullapool's waterway), and the trade was particularly popular with fishermen from the Eastern Bloc. The Klondyker trade peaked in 1985 when 94 per cent of the overall catch was transferred to foreign vessels (150,273 tons of mackerel worth £16.5 million).[37]

The social impact of Ullapool's popularity with the Klondykers was significant, but, as in Dunoon, it was not straightforward. Local memories of Eastern European Klondykers today present them as welcome guests, and the village's hospitality was often rewarded with gifts from behind the Iron Curtain. Contemporary records, however, suggest that relations were not always positive.

Although the influx of seamen ashore from Eastern European ships moored in Loch Broom ensured that the autumn and winter months were not fallow after the tourist season, the growth of business was not welcomed by everyone. Local fishermen who did not sell to the Klondykers feared that they would be driven out of business; others bemoaned the poor behaviour of visiting sailors; and many, including local politicians, were worried about the environmental impact of these processing ships dumping rubbish and diesel fuel into the loch.

However, local onshore businesses undoubtedly profited from doing business with the ships. Shops, cafés and pubs in the village were frequented by overseas crewmen and officers, who purchased items for their stay aboard the Klondykers, and for their families and friends at home. Some bought electrical and bulkier items from mail-order catalogues via the shops in Ullapool, while others boarded coaches to Inverness for shopping trips.

The character of the Russian seaman Viktor in the acclaimed film *Local Hero* (1983) may have been a caricature, but the villagers' fondness for him and the exchange of goods, services and culture he portrayed, certainly evokes the exchange between Scottish locals and Eastern European traders at the

Kaliningrad Fishing Corporation ship pennants

Kaliningrad Fishing Corporation ship pennants gifted to Ullapool locals by visiting seamen. The Soviet visitors and Scottish locals often exchanged goods.

© Ullapool Museum Trust

Soviet ship moored at Ullapool

Between the 1970s and 1990s, Ullapool on Scotland's north-west coast attracted 'Klondyker' fishermen from the Soviet Union. They processed herring on board large fishing vessels to be taken back to the Soviet Union.

© Ullapool Museum Trust

time of the Klondykers. Indeed, when shopkeeper Mrs Wyatt hails Viktor over the radio with 'Welcome to democracy, boatman!' there is an air of truth to her statement (albeit Hollywood-filtered). Ullapool's local community may well have developed a special sense of the differences between Western and Eastern economies from the seamen's rusty and outdated ships and equipment, and their propensity for chocolate and consumer goods.

By the late 1980s, the difficulties experienced in communist economies were evident in the ways that Eastern Bloc fishermen approached the trade – often bartering frozen white fish for mackerel, or striking up deals whereby they offered to process catches for other foreign vessels (from Japan or Brazil for instance) in exchange for a small percentage of the fish. Ullapooler locals certainly witnessed global economics playing out on Loch Broom.

Behind the Curtain

While citizens of the superpowers travelled to Scotland, tourism from Scotland to the Soviet Union – perhaps unexpectedly – continued throughout the Cold War. Companies offered package holidays behind the Iron Curtain for those interested in learning about Soviet arts, culture and lifestyle. In Scotland, this trade expanded significantly after 1961 when the Scotland-USSR Society established the travel company Sovscot Tours Limited. Records suggest that Sovscot Tours had up to 3000 registered holiday-makers, plus an equal number of visitors who had booked reciprocal holidays from the USSR to Scotland.

The Scotland-USSR Society believed that such trips were beneficial to Cold War co-operation and peace:

> The impressions so created may not lead to an [sic] unanimity of views on the superiority of one or other social system, but certainly counteract the worst causes of antagonism. It becomes clear that people on both sides of the East-West divide have the same everyday experiences, hopes and dreams.[38]

One enthusiastic traveller, Eileen Crowford, embarked on a series of holidays that took her not only to major cities including Moscow and Leningrad (today's St Petersburg), but all over the Eastern Bloc, from the German Democratic Republic to Romania, the Central Asian Republics to Yugoslavia. While on holiday, Crowford went on excursions, intended to show visitors an exciting and positive view of communist societies.

These tours provided opportunities to purchase or barter for local goods, souvenirs and memorabilia. Crowford was an astute and prolific buyer, her souvenir collection represents not only what a Scottish tourist may have wished to obtain from a trip abroad, but also what Soviet countries may have wanted to portray of their national identity to the outside world. Her collection also reflected her own political convictions and how she engaged with communist culture and politics.[39]

While it is not clear if Crowford was a Communist Party member, she was certainly a Communist sympathiser and a Sovietophile. She was also a member of the Scotland-USSR Society, which gave her ample opportunity to attend the arts, culture and educational events staged by its organisers as part of their Soviet friendship programme. Crowford's extensive archive documents not only her trips, but her independent research on Soviet communist countries. It contextualises the low value, but carefully chosen, items that she brought home from the Eastern Bloc, which are recorded as reminders of her journeys.

For example, Crowford collected many *znachki*. These were mass-produced Soviet lapel badges with important events and emblems of cultural significance depicted on their metal surfaces. The political and economic cultures underpinning *znachki* ownership evolved with changes to successive state ideologies. Soviet people were thus encouraged to be collectors of *znachki* and the badges became a unique state-sanctioned mass-produced consumer product.

At the same time, with international interest in Soviet achievements increasing, *znachki* took on a new role as souvenirs of Soviet advancement in areas like the Space Race. Crowford collected several types, from the niche commemorative badge of the youth division of the Water Rescue Society to a badge honouring the anniversary of the October Revolution.

Even the act of purchasing *znachki*, postcards, mementoes, excursion tickets, and so on, would have confronted her directly with the very different economic system that governed communist societies. Crowford would not have been able simply to purchase all her shopping freely in local currency – only some of the items in her collection would have been bought in rubles. Her souvenirs would also have been acquired in state-run shops, often within her hotel, which accepted traveller's cheques or 'hard' foreign currency. Sometimes shopkeepers were even known to barter for consumer goods like chewing gum.

Eileen Crowford recorded her holiday encounters in meticulous detail, but with little attention to her own feelings, experiences and views. While this makes it difficult to gain her impression of life in both Scotland and the Soviet Union during the Cold War, it can be gleaned from her travels and material collections that Scottish interest in the Soviet way of life was strong.

In direct contrast to the individual travel of tourists like Crowford, there were formal state visits from the Soviet Union to Scotland. Diplomatic travel provided a barometer of the Cold War temperature and connected Scots with élite-level politics through local visits and place-based interactions. The Soviet Premiers Nikita Khrushchev, Alexei Kosygin and Mikael Gorbachev all visited Scotland at points during the Cold War, as well as numerous other state officials and cultural ambassadors.

Each visit provided an opportunity to present a version of Soviet communism to the public while gaining an understanding of Britain, its politics, industries and culture. Although they followed an itinerary of predictable state formalities, with engagements at the Palace of Holyroodhouse and the Scottish National War Memorial, for example, such visits also produced unusual instances of cultural connection whereby Scottish places and people entered the limelight unexpectedly.

On Saturday 11 February 1967, the Soviet Union Premier Alexei Kosygin arrived in Glasgow for a weekend tour. Having spent five busy days in London with Prime Minister Harold Wilson discussing how American negotiations on the Vietnam War should proceed, Kosygin's visit to Scotland provided a welcome break.[40] Accompanied by the Soviet Ambassador to the United Kingdom, he was greeted by hundreds of onlookers in George Square when he arrived in Glasgow. He then visited the Hunterston nuclear power station in Ayrshire (see page 32).

Kosygin even managed to fit in a football match at Rugby Park – the home ground of Kilmarnock Football Club – where he watched Rangers FC win 2–1.[41] This sporting detour may well have been connected to the Scottish Secretary of State Willie Ross's support for Kilmarnock – his hometown and parliamentary seat. In preparation for Kosygin's arrival, Kilmarnock FC flew the Soviet flag above the ground and the match programme declared, 'History is made at Rugby Park this afternoon when, for the first time, a Russian Prime Minister will watch a football match in Scotland. Kilmarnock FC extends a hearty welcome to Mr. Alexei Kosygin and hope he will enjoy the match.'[42]

Optimising the photo opportunities, before kick-off, Kosygin met every team member on the pitch and presented both captains with a glass globe trophy which remain in the possession of each club. He was also invited to check the ball with the referee before the match began and sat, accompanied by his daughter, in the Director's box, flanked by the club chairman William McIvor and other local dignitaries. One enthusiastic supporter was photographed handing Kosygin a handmade tartan tammie from the fans' enclosure.

During a session of the House of Commons the following week, Harold Wilson noted that Kosygin had spoken in 'glowing terms' of his Scottish tour, to the extent that the latter had proposed the twinning of places in Scotland with towns in the Soviet Union. Meanwhile, the South Ayrshire MP Emrys Hughes took the opportunity to reflect not only on the success

Eileen Crowford

Edinburgh resident Eileen Crowford began visiting Eastern Europe in the 1950s and continued beyond her retirement from her position as a secretary at Edinburgh City Council in 1973.

Her trips to the German Democratic Republic, the Soviet Union and Romania were often arranged through specialist tour operators such as Sovscot Tours Limited. This Glasgow-based travel agent was founded by the Scotland-USSR Society in 1961 to facilitate trips for thousands of Scots to the Soviet Union during the Cold War.

Foreign visitors were encouraged by tour guides to buy souvenirs from street vendors or through official Berozka shops in exchange for foreign currency. Crowford bought hundreds of souvenirs over the years, including jewellery and medals related to places she had visited, as well as political badges.

After her death in 1990, she left her collection of Soviet souvenirs and ephemera to National Museums Scotland. This collection offers a fascinating insight into the friendly exchanges between the East and West throughout the Cold War.

Top to bottom:

Gold-coloured metal badge from Samarkand with the hammer and sickle of the USSR, *c.* **1970s**

Soviet badge representing a lifeboat organisation

Hotel card, St Petersburg, August 1973

Right: One ruble banknote belonging to Miss Crowford

Images © National Museums Scotland

Balkan Holidays
Autumn, Winter & Spring 1977-78
Ski-ing, Coach, Two-Country & Stay-Put Holidays
City Breaks, Xmas & Easter Specials

Balkan Holidays Limited travel brochure, Autumn, Winter 1977 and Spring 1978

Image © National Museums Scotland

of Scotland as a host country, but wondered whether this proved a 'real wish that this should be the beginning of the end of the arms race and the cold war'.[43]

Cold War conversations

Kosygin's visit to the football match was not the only diplomatic connection between the Soviet Union and Scotland. John Erickson, a Scottish academic, played an important role in facilitating conversations across the Iron Curtain.

Erickson, Professor of Higher Defence Studies at the University of Edinburgh from 1969, was a leading historian whose research focused on the Soviet military command as well as the Soviet Union during the Second World War.[44] The respect his research had garnered among academicians of the Soviet Academy of Sciences allowed Erickson unique access to some of the Second World War generals and to Soviet archives. Because of his position at the University of Edinburgh, his linguistic abilities and expertise in Soviet strategy and tactics, he became increasingly interested in issues of arms control over the 1970s – how to manage the nuclear race arms race between the United States and the Soviet Union.

The origin of a series of conferences, known as the Edinburgh Conversations, offers a snapshot into how Scottish and UK élite networks academia and the geopolitical climate all came together at that time. They also show how the increase of tensions resulted in the tightening of connec-

Soviet Premier Alexei Kosygin on tour in Scotland

In 1967, Soviet Premier Alexei Kosygin was taken on a whistle-stop tour of Scotland. This image shows Mr Kosygin on the pitch presenting players with a glass trophy.

© The Scotsman Publications. Licensor www.SCRAN.ac.uk

Opposite: Conversations in Scotland

In November 1984, the University of Edinburgh's Professor John Erickson, Dr Georgiy Golitsyn from the USSR Academy of Sciences, and Professor Paul Ehrlich of Stanford University (left to right) attended the 'Nuclear Winter' conference in Glasgow. The conference discussed nuclear weapons and their environmental impact.

© The Scotsman Publications. Licensor www.SCRAN.ac.uk

tions between Scotland, the United Kingdom and the Soviet Union during the last decade of the Cold War in the 1980s.

Connections across the Iron Curtain had weakened during the late 1970s and early 1980s as the nuclear arms race accelerated and both the Soviet Union and NATO deployed new generations of medium-range nuclear missiles. The United Kingdom and other Western countries broke off formal diplomatic relations with the Soviet Union in the wake of the invasion of Afghanistan (1979), but there were those who wished to keep informal networks in place.

In 1980, the famous science journalist Peter (Lord) Ritchie Calder travelled to Moscow, as chair of the Scotland-USSR Society, to discuss the issues of the arms race, as well as the Soviet Union's poor record of human rights. The welcome was frosty and the discussions almost hostile. Nonetheless, Calder heard that the Soviets wanted to continue conversations and he consulted with Erickson, among others, on the matter of a follow-up visit by Scottish academics. Erickson, who also had excellent connections to the American defence establishment because of his work on arms control, became part of that delegation.

Erickson met with the Deputy Chairman of the Soviet Communist Party's Foreign Affairs Committee, Vadim Zagladin, and together they began to plan subsequent meetings. In discussions with the University of Edinburgh's Principal, John Burnett, Erickson proposed to keep these relations alive through informal exchanges between Scots and their counterparts in the Soviet Union.

Meetings alternated annually between Edinburgh and the Soviet Union from 1981 until 1988. These were founded on the assumption, common to what has been called 'scientific internationalism', that scientists and other scholars would be able to discuss controversial issues beyond ideological, political or cultural boundaries because they all shared an interest in finding out the truth. In the case of John Erickson – apart from his in-depth knowledge of Soviet military affairs in the past and present – his personal distance from political office and his physical distance from Whitehall were perhaps reasons for his ready acceptance in official Soviet circles.[45]

The first meeting, held in Edinburgh in early October 1981, addressed the theme of 'Survival in the Nuclear Age'. As a University of Edinburgh press statement declared, the aim was to 'explore through professional exchanges the issues arising from the realities and dangers of the nuclear age, by means of private informal discussions between informed individuals from Scotland and Russia'.[46]

Erickson was the main speaker of the British delegation, which was led by Lord Calder and John Burnett. Sir Hugh Beach, a retired British general and former commandant of the Army Staff College, was another British participant. The Soviet side was headed by Professor Vitaly Kobysh, who was linked to the Department of International Information of the Soviet Communist Party.

The second, somewhat fraught, meeting took place in Moscow in the autumn of 1982. Erickson led a group of high-profile academics, military officers and trade union officials, including the international lawyer Professor Iain McGibbon from Edinburgh, the ecologist Dr John Loraine, also from Edinburgh, Field Marshall Lord Carver, the former Chief of Defence Staff, Lord Calder's son Nigel, a historian, and the American Colonel Lynn Hansen, a US Air Force officer with an interest in arms control and a former student of Erickson.

The 1982 Soviet delegation was led by Gennadi Yanaev, Deputy President of the Union of Soviet Friendship Societies, Major General Konstantin Mikhailov from the Soviet General Staff, and Georgi Arbatov, one of the leading Soviet experts on American politics.

As in the second meeting, the third one in Edinburgh (September 1983) was overshadowed by mutual accusations about the responsibility for the worsening of the international climate. It took place during a time of crisis and fears of a hot war that followed the shooting down of a South Korean civilian plane by the Soviet Air Force due to a navigational error over the Pacific earlier that month. The incident cost the lives of more than 260 people

Participants this time included Eugene Rostow, the former Director of the American Arms Control and Disarmament Agency, and Vice Admiral Sir Ian McGeoch, a former Flag Officer Scotland and Northern Ireland.

The British delegation to the meeting in Moscow in 1984 included the Conservative MP Nicholas Soames, grandson of Winston Churchill, and James Eberle, Director of the Royal Institute of International Affairs.

By this time the Edinburgh Conversations had taken on a more formal character. Similar to the smaller-scale Pugwash Conferences, which brought together scientists from around the world and across the blocs to discuss issues relating to the nuclear arms race, the Edinburgh Conversations became unofficial diplomatic forums. Scientists, technical experts and diplomats addressed arms control and the environment, most significantly after the meltdown of the nuclear reactor of Chernobyl in the Ukrainian Soviet Republic in April 1986.

In the late 1980s, the meetings became directly concerned with drafting international communication on arms control and nuclear weapons in Europe, providing an informal channel through which the Soviet Union, the United Kingdom and the United States cleared technical hurdles and sounded out options before the official treaty negotiations began.

In 1989, the British Government decided to end the initiative, arguing that developments on the ground – the process of liberalisation in Eastern Europe and the Soviet Union that would ultimately lead to the collapse of the Iron Curtain and the end of the Cold War – had overtaken the usefulness of the meetings.

Overall, the Conversations, though not without controversy, highlighted that communication across the Cold War divide was possible and could be constructive. In a context of heightened nuclear anxiety – particularly on the Soviet side – such discussions offered an important avenue for building trust; and proved that informal, non-governmental initiatives could provide important connections during a time of heightened tension.

In a different Edinburgh institution – St John the Evangelist Episcopal Church – another group began to engage with early 1980s international politics. This time however, it was in a creative and highly public manner. Mural artists Paul Grime and Michael Greenlaw, inspired by the community arts movement epitomised by the Craigmillar Festival Society, embarked on painting a series of arresting and polemical paintings on a wall outside the church.

The rector of St John's, Neville Chamberlain, played a crucial role in supporting the production of these works by Grime and Greenlaw, although their contents jarred with his congregation's sensibilities. Chamberlain took a risk by allowing the 'Artists for Justice and Peace' (as Grime and Greenlaw dubbed their initiative) the freedom to portray complex and controversial topics through raw imagery.

The murals highlighted topics from 'International Aid for Africa' to 'South African Apartheid', and frequently referred to Cold War-related competition between East and West. By linking questions of the arms race to issues of social justice, the murals connected the nuclear threat that mainly affected Europe and North Atlantic countries with the legacies of colonialism and international development that characterised the global Cold War.

Although, as noted above (see page 68), the churches in general could sometimes play a leading role in anti-communist rhetoric, clerics were also engaged at the forefront of Cold War reconciliation activities. Chamberlain was not the only Scottish religious leader to advocate justice and peace during the Cold War period. Canon Kenyon Wright, the Scottish Episcopalian priest known primarily for his efforts to establish a Scottish Constitutional Convention, also had an energetic approach to relationship-building with Warsaw Pact nations throughout the Cold War. Wright began his peace campaigning in 1960 when he joined the anti-Polaris CND march at Faslane. As the Cold War continued, he participated in the Christian Peace Conference – a group of delegates committed to improving communication across the East–West divide and encouraging collaboration. Scotland and Scots were instrumental in Cold War dialogues.

Peace and war

These efforts for peace were no doubt fuelled by the ever-present threat of war. When the protagonists of the film *Local Hero* look up at the sky as RAF Tornados fly past, menacingly low and searingly loud, the audience is reminded of the permanent presence of Cold War technology in even the most unlikely of Scottish landscapes. Similarly, in the novel *Greenvoe* (1972), when the inhabitants of the fictional eponymous village accept the arrival of 'Operation Black Star' and its unexplained but eviscerating construction plans, author George Mackay Brown evokes the ever-present, sometimes invasive and intrusive presence of the industrial military complex in far-flung Scottish regions.

By assessing the connections between Scottish individuals and communities with their international counterparts we can view more clearly how Scottish society experienced and responded to the Cold War.

Whether through youthful optimism, arts and cultural interests, sporting fandom, working-class solidarity or political impulse, Scottish civilians connected with Cold War issues and often actively participated in bridging its divide. Human encounters illustrate the extent to which the Cold War influenced individuals' lives. Scots engaged with international issues such as political persecution, economic challenges and alternative social structures in a way that also allowed them to evaluate and reflect on their own experiences at home in Scottish society.

Bread Not Bombs mural, St John the Evangelist Episcopal Church, Edinburgh

Since 1982, St John's Episcopal Church on Princes Street, Edinburgh, has produced murals based on issues of concern to the church and the wider society. Artists for Justice and Peace, such as Paul Grime and Michael Greenlaw, painted a series of murals including Bread Not Bombs in 1986.

Courtesy of Paul Grime

Notes

1. Nathan Hennebry, 'Scottish trade unionists in Ukraine, 1951', originally published in *Challenge*, magazine of the Young Communist League of Britain. Available at: https://challenge-magazine.org/2023/01/14/scottish-trade-unionists-in-ukraine-1951/.
2. https://scottish-finnish-society.org.uk/about.
3. Jim Phillips, *Scottish Coal Miners in the Twentieth Century* (Edinburgh: Edinburgh University Press, 2019).
4. Ewan Gibbs, *Coal Country: The Meaning and Memory of Deindustrialization in Postwar Scotland* (London: University of London Press, 2021).
5. Sean Creighton, *Politics and culture: Paul Robeson in the UK* (London: History & Social Action, 2013).
6. BFI film archive, 'Paul Robeson sings to Scottish miners (1949)', www.youtube.com.
7. Patrick Russell, 'Memories from the mine: the day I filmed Paul Robeson', British Film Institute blog post, 24 January 2017, www.bfi.org.uk.
8. Tony Perucci, 'The Red Mask of Sanity: Paul Robeson, HUAC, and the Sound of Cold War Performance', *The Drama Review* 53 (2009), pp. 18–48.
9. Robeson in the *Evening Dispatch*, quoted in Gerald Horne, *Paul Robeson: The Artist as Revolutionary* (London: Pluto Press, 2016), p. 174.
10. British Pathé Film Archive, 'Robeson Leads May Day Parade', 1960, www.britishpathe.com.
11. Horne, *Paul Robeson*, 2016.
12. National Library of Scotland, PB9.217.27/4.
13. Scott Lyall, 'MacDiarmid, communism and the poetry of commitment', in Scott Lyall and Margery Palmer McCulloch (eds), *The Edinburgh Companion to Hugh MacDiarmid*, 2011, pp. 68–81.
14. Ronald Paul, 'Scotland's Independence and the Poetry of Hugh MacDiarmid', *Socialism and Democracy* 35 (2020), pp. 79–91.
15. Tony Howard and Liz Wood, 'Let Robeson Sing', 2009, https://warwick.ac.uk/services/library/mrc.
16. Cited in Angela Bartie, *The Edinburgh Festivals: Culture and Society in Post-war Britain* (Edinburgh: Edinburgh University Press, 2013), pp. 47, 51. From *The Times*, 22 August 1949 and ECL, *Submissions on Behalf of Edinburgh Festival Society for Nobel Peace Prize* respectively.
17. Cited in Bartie, *The Edinburgh Festivals*, p. 66.
18. Cited in Bartie, *The Edinburgh Festivals*.
19. Quoted in Bartie, *The Edinburgh Festivals*, pp. 86, 89. From *The Times*, 22 May 1958 and *Edinburgh Evening News*, 17 May 1956 respectively.
20. Jim Gledhill, 'Breaking the Ice: When Hugh MacDiarmid met Yevgeny Yevtushenko', 2022, https://blog.nms.ac.uk.
21. Pamphlet, *Vote for Dr. C. M. Grieve* (Hugh MacDiarmid); Communist candidate (Strathearn Institute, 1964), National Library of Scotland General Collections, 1968.220.
22. Cited in Bartie, *The Edinburgh Festivals*, p. 103. From the International Writer's Conference, August 1962, original transcript, Day 2, pp. 4–10.
23. Quoted in Bartie, *The Edinburgh Festivals*, pp. 103, 104.
24. *Scotland-USSR Society, 1945–1985: 40 Years Working For Friendship* (Glasgow: Scotland-USSR Society, 1985), p. 9. We are grateful to the 'Scotland-Russia: Cultural Encounters Since 1900' project at the University of Edinburgh for access to these papers.
25. Central Intelligence Agency, 'Soviet-Sponsored Societies of Friendship and Cultural Relations', October 1957, p. vi, available at: https://www.cia.gov/readingroom/docs/CIA-RDP78-00915R000800190022-9.pdf.
26. Quoted in Thomas Kernberg, *The Polish Community in Scotland*, PhD thesis, University of Glasgow, 1990, p. 329.
27. Graeme Strachan, 'How the north-east of Scotland became a target for the Stasi at the height of the Cold War', *The Courier*, 2 September 2020.
28. George G. Giarchi, *Between McAlpine and Polaris* (London: Routledge, 2021 [1984]).
29. *Glasgow Evening Times*, January 1962.
30. *Glasgow Evening Times*, March 1963.
31. Giarchi, *McAlpine and Polaris*, 2021, pp. 247, 178.
32. *Glasgow Evening Times*, March 1963.
33. Andrene Messersmith, *The American Years: Dunoon and the US Navy* (Glendaruel: Argyll Publishing 2023), p. 43.
34. Quoted in Messersmith, *The American Years*, 2023, p. 75.
35. J. M. Moss to T. C. S. Stitt, 15 September 1977, National Records of Scotland, AF62/5969.
36. M. J. MacLeod to Miss Ross, 13 July 1977, National Records of Scotland, AF62/5969.
37. Don Shaw, *Ullapool and the Klondykers: A Unique Era in Lochbroom* (Ullapool: Shaw, 2011).
38. *Scotland-USSR Society, 1945–198*, 1985, p. 9. We are grateful to the 'Scotland-Russia: Cultural Encounters Since 1900' project at the University of Edinburgh for access to these papers.
39. Carys Wilkins, 'Holidaying behind the Iron Curtain: The material culture of tourism in Cold War Eastern Europe', *Matkailututkimus* 17 (2022), pp. 53–71.
40. Geraint Hughes, 'A "missed opportunity" for peace? Harold Wilson, British diplomacy, and the sunflower initiative to end the Vietnam war, February 1967', *Diplomacy & Statecraft* 14 (2003), pp. 106–130.
41. British Pathé Film Archive, 'Kosygin Visits Nuclear Power Station', 1967, www.britishpathe.com.
42. Official Programme, Kilmarnock Football Club, Saturday 11 February 1967. Access courtesy of Kilmarnock Football Club archives and museum.
43. 'Mr Kosygin (visit)', Hansard, HC, Parliamentary Debates, vol. 741, cols 116–115, 13 February 1967.
44. Malcolm Mackintosh, 'John Erickson, 1929–2002', in P. J. Marshall (ed.), *Proceedings of the British Academy, Volume 124. Biographical Memoirs of Fellows*, III, 2005.
45. Comment by Michael Howard in Foreword to Ljubica Erickson and Mark Erickson (eds), *Russia: War, Peace and Diplomacy. Essays in Honour of John Erickson*, 2004, p. viii.
46. University of Edinburgh Press Information, 'Survival in a Nuclear Age: The 'Edinburgh Conversations' with Russian Experts', 5 October 1981.

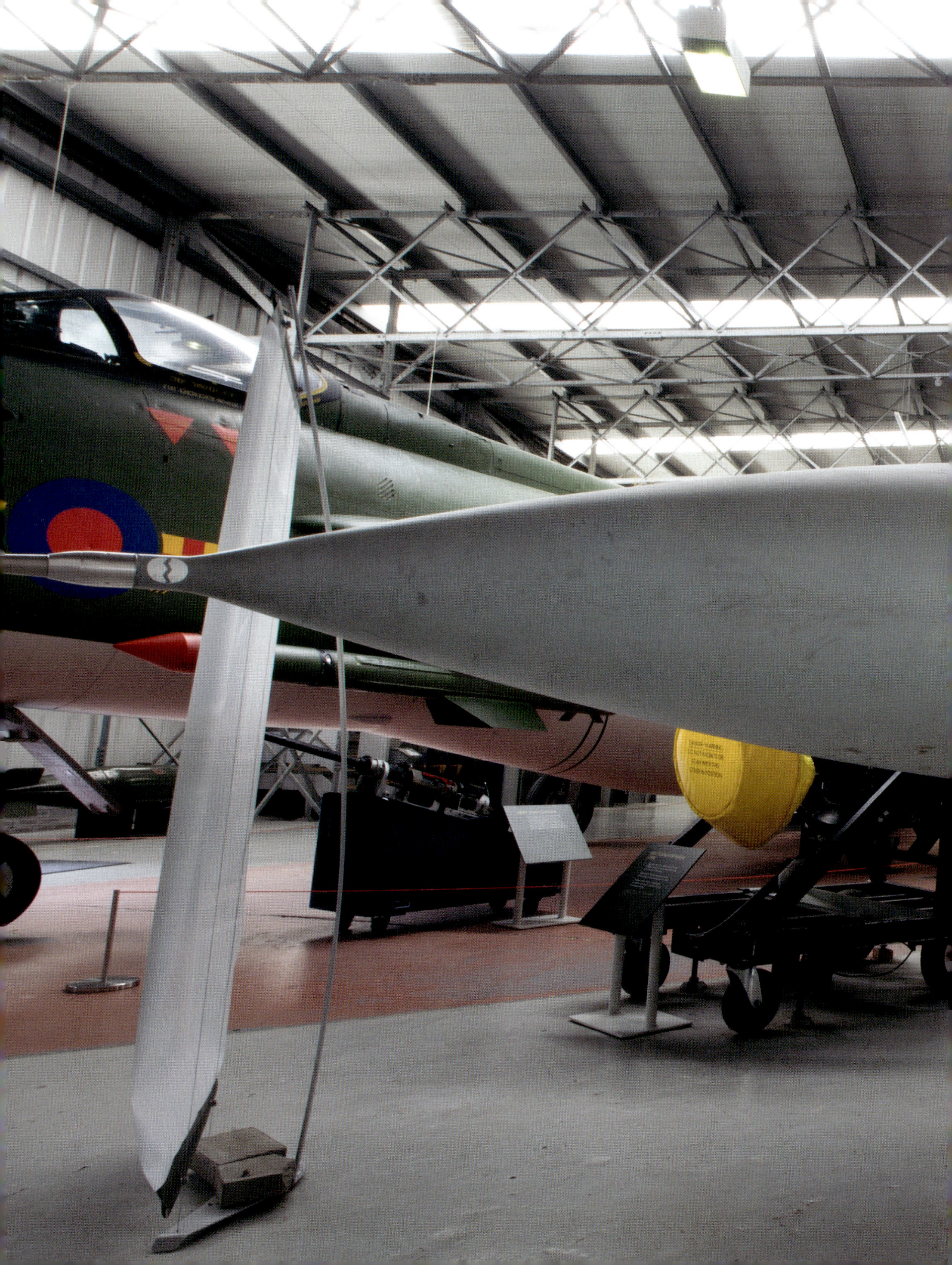

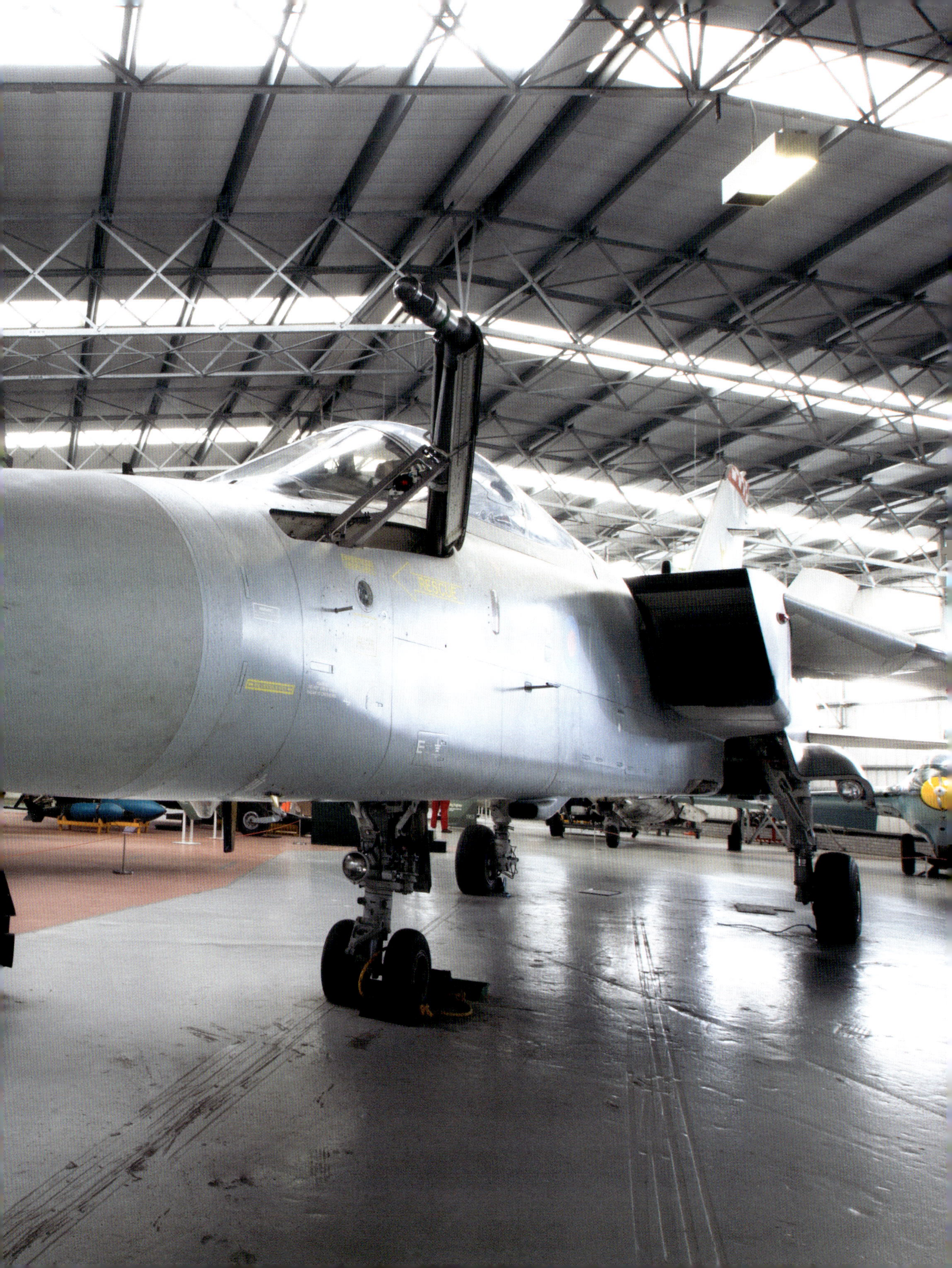
RESCUE

Chapter 4

Material memories

In August 1963, a Royal Air Force Vulcan nuclear bomber numbered XM597 entered service. It joined one of the 160 aircraft of the V-force nuclear deterrent bombing fleet that had been on Quick Reaction Alert the year before during the Cuban Missile Crisis. Fortunately, during six years as part of Britain's first line of nuclear defence, XM597 was never called upon, nor were its Blue Steel nuclear missiles ever used.

Later converted to deploy conventional weapons, XM597 did however take part in the Falklands Conflict.[1] It became part of Scotland's Cold War heritage when it landed at East Fortune airfield near Edinburgh in April 1984. There the bomber joined the collection of the National Museum of Flight, which was expanding into the hangars and other buildings bordering the airstrip. The runway had been extended to accommodate American bombers (though they never arrived) and the hangars had been used to store supplies in readiness for nuclear attack.

The ageing aircraft's arrival, and its new home at East Fortune, illustrate two important points about the impact of the Cold War on Scotland. First, that the material culture of the imaginary war became heritage even before the Cold War ended, and continues to be an important way to access the experience of the conflict; and second, that the built environment of warfare and readiness has left its marks on the Scottish landscape. Military bases, bunkers and communication technology remain with us today.

This chapter will show that the experience of the Cold War in Scotland continues via its legacies in topography, buildings and objects. It may have been an 'imaginary war' in the United Kingdom, but there are real, material reminders of what archaeologists have dubbed its 'fearsome heritage'.[2] Whereas some of the topics of this book have been at the level of global politics, the everyday experience of Scotland's Cold War happened in specific places with specific things. Geography and objects provoke memories of the Cold War.

Pages 106–7: Panavia Tornado

Ferranti in Edinburgh was involved in developing avionics for the Panavia Tornado aircraft for the RAF in the late 1980s. The wings of this aircraft could move forward to provide extra lift at low speeds, and then backwards for supersonic flight.

Image © National Museums Scotland

What remains

Scotland was physically changed by the Cold War. The military presence endowed the country with the remains of radar stations, monitoring posts, anti-aircraft defences, missile installations, airfields, nuclear bunkers and submarine depots. One researcher considered these 'Cold War obelisk[s] honouring Scotland's contributions at the time'.[3] Many of them were repurposed from the Second World War, but by the end of the 1980s the staggering scale of infrastructure investment had left an unprecedented change on the landscape.

Many of their strange shapes, surrounded by fences and barbed wire, survive to this day. As photographer Alex Boyd notes, this 'Scottish Military Pastoral'

> … can be found across the country if we are willing to look for it. From military roads, checkpoints and barracks to warning signage, rocket launch lamps, red flags, and the imposing radar domes which dominate the landscapes of South Clettreval, Galloway, and St Kilda, Scotland is a landscape which is heavily militarised.[4]

Most obvious are the submarine bases and their accompanying support facilities, because many are still in use to accommodate the Trident fleet. The base at Faslane is not only a vestige of the Cold War but, alongside the Coulport facility, as His Majesty's Naval Base (HMNB) Clyde, is the main naval presence in Scotland. It supports the Vanguard-class Trident-armed submarine flotilla as well as hunter-killer boats.

Rosyth Dockyard, by contrast, does not house active nuclear boats but their remaining predecessors. The facility was used for refitting and maintenance throughout the Cold War until 2003, but boats are decommissioned there now – or rather, they would be if the timescales and costs were not so astronomical. And so, seven nuclear submarines float in the dockyard awaiting their fate, a reminder of the nuclear role Scotland played during the Cold War. Although no longer fuelled, their continued radiation risk is a reminder of the fears during the conflict. HMS *Dreadnought* has now been awaiting decommissioning at Rosyth since 1980 – many times longer than its active service life.

Even the protests against these sites have had a lasting impact. The Faslane peace camp still endures over forty years on, the longest continuously occupied site of its kind in the world. It comprises a small number of makeshift buildings, caravans and disused vehicles; and in October 2023 residents installed a plaque in the peace garden at the camp, by way of a memorial for victims of UK nuclear testing in Australia. Glasgow Museums now has a caravan from the camp in its collection.

Cold War infrastructure is also evident beyond the Central Belt, at the topographical extremes of the country. The remains of RAF Aird Uig can be found on the west coast of the Isle of Lewis. Built in 1954 as a radar station, it was originally part of the ROTOR early warning air defence radar system intended to detect Soviet bombers. The base housed nearly 200 personnel in more than twenty buildings at its peak.

At the far north-east of Scotland, on top of a hill in Unst, Shetland – parallel with Alaska and north of what was then known as Leningrad – is the looming radome of Remote Radar Head Saxa Vord.[5] Originating in the Second World War and upgraded in the 1950s, at its peak it was of a similar scale to Aird Uig – which was significant on an island with some 700

Vulcan bomber

Background: Avro Vulcan B.2A XM597 at the National Museum of Flight, East Fortune

Image © National Museums Scotland

Inset: Three advanced jets known as the V-force (from top): the Handley Page Victor, Avro Vulcan and Vickers Valiant.

Keystone Press / Alamy Stock Photo

In 1947 the British Air Ministry identified the need for heavy bombers to dispatch the nuclear weapons under development and so commissioned a fleet of nuclear-capable jet bombers. These became the 'V-force': the Vickers Valiant, the Handley Page Victor and the Avro Vulcan.

The latter was a striking Delta-winged aircraft with a crew of five and a 34-metre wingspan. It had the capacity to deliver Blue Steel missiles with Red Snow thermonuclear warheads and was infamous for the howl generated by its four Olympus engines.

During the 1960s the V-force was central to the British nuclear deterrent, but after technical developments on both sides of the Iron Curtain, this responsibility shifted to submarines in 1969. Vulcans were then adapted to carry ballistic missiles (that is, non-nuclear), and in 1982 several took part in the 'Black Buck' long-range bombing missions to the Falkland Islands.

Otherwise, the 140-strong V-force was largely scrapped during the 1980s. Nineteen Vulcans survive as heritage, including XM597, a popular attraction at the National Museum of Flight. Parked in the Scottish landscape, never to howl again, this Vulcan is not only a Falklands veteran but also a giant memento of the Cold War airborne stand-off.

Faslane caravan

The Faslane peace camp was established in 1982 in response to the UK Government's purchase of Trident missiles from the United States. This colourful caravan adorned with peace messaging was originally part of the Faslane camp and was later donated to Glasgow Museums.

Mike Booth / Alamy Stock Photo

Above: RAF Aird Uig

RAF Aird Uig on the west coast of the Isle of Lewis. Built in 1954 as a radar station, it was originally part of the ROTOR 3 early warning air defence radar system intended to detect Soviet bombers.

UrbanImages / Alamy Stock Photo

Left: Blast doors from AAOR East Kilbride

The blast doors from the 1950s Anti-Aircraft Operations Room, an underground bunker in East Kilbride. This bunker became the Scottish Civil Defence Western Zone Control base in the 1960s and later the Western Zone Regional Government Headquarters.

Image © National Museums Scotland

Remote Radar Head Saxa Vord

The Remote Radar Head Saxa Vord in Unst, Shetland, was also part of the ROTOR radar network.

Alain Le Garsmeur Secret Landscapes / Alamy Stock Photo

residents.[6] Having closed in 2006, the Ministry of Defence decided in 2017 to reopen Saxa Vord as a fully operational radar station in response to increased Soviet activities. The station has been active again since 2019.

Remains of the Anti-Aircraft Operations Rooms (AAOR) are additional legacies of the warning and response network developed in tandem with ROTOR in the 1950s. Across Britain, 31 two-storey or semi-sunken structures were built. Scotland houses four: at Gairloch in Wester Ross, Inverkip in Inverclyde, Craigiehall near Edinburgh, and in the grounds of Torrance House at East Kilbride near Glasgow.

Some operations rooms were repurposed and became part of the extensive civilian infrastructure. There is a considerable legacy of the network of war rooms and civil defence structures, political headquarters and emergency storage facilities. Underneath Barnton Quarry near Edinburgh, for example, is a large complex whose history is telling of the changing approaches taken by the UK Government during the conflict.[7]

Used during the Second World War for RAF Fighter Command operations, in the early 1950s a new three-storey bunker with three-metre concrete walls was constructed in the quarry as a Sector Operations Centre for collating radar information from across Scotland. Passed to the Scottish Home and Health Department in the 1960s, it was the headquarters of the Scottish Regional Seats of Government, with the capacity to accommodate 400 officials and politicians and supplies to last for up to a month. Lothian Regional Council then took it over in the 1980s; in 2021 Historic Environment Scotland awarded it Category A listed building status.

The Anti-Aircraft Operations Rooms mentioned above were also redeployed for political and civil defence purposes after the Anti-Aircraft Command was disbanded. Other surviving bunkers followed a similar administrative journey. The three-storey structure in Inverness was built in 1941 as a radar command centre: it was used for training in the early Cold War, then for civil defence, Royal Observer Corps (ROC) and, in the 1980s, extended to be an emergency centre for the Highland Regional Council. Attempts have been underway to make it a museum.

More successful in the latter respect is 'Scotland's Secret Bunker' in Fife. Built for ROTOR, the British air defence radar system, in 1953 under a bungalow of similar design to other radar operations centres, it was later adapted for civil defence, a subsidiary Regional Seat of Government, and is now an active visitor attraction.[8]

For a time, Barnton Quarry had housed the Royal Observer Corps. Not always so obvious, but nonetheless widespread, are the remains of their monitoring system. Many posts were housed in prefabricated reinforced concrete structures of around five by two metres. Among the twenty or so underground monitoring posts and the larger Groups headquarters that survive, an extensive example can be found in Craigiebarns in Dundee, which housed the 28 Group Headquarters. It originally opened in 1962, then was later extended as the UK Warning and Monitoring Organisation (UKWMO) Caledonian Sector headquarters, stretching over three floors. Veteran observers and other enthusiasts are now restoring the building.

The surviving Cold War-built environment extends into industrial remains. This is especially evident in power generation.[9] Despite the grand plans of a nuclear future, only four nuclear power facilities were constructed in Scotland. While Torness remains operational, the long process of decommissioning has begun at Dounreay, Chapelcross and Hunterston. It will take decades and many of the surviving structures will endure.

Radioactive waste from atomic sites has left a long-lasting impact on the Scottish landscape. Its presence will affect Scottish lives – where houses can be built, which beaches can be walked on and where fish can be caught – for hundreds of years. The multi-billion pound programme of rendering these sites and their surrounding landscape safe is controlled by the Nuclear Decommissioning Authority which now stores its extensive archive at 'Nucleus' near Wick, Caithness, not far from Dounreay. Torness, meanwhile, continues to provide power (at the time of writing, and although the Scottish Government is opposed to new nuclear power, it plans to extend Torness' life).[10]

What unites Torness and Faslane, Barnton Quarry and Saxa Vord, as well as many other buildings, ruins and sites, is one particular material: concrete. The industrial historian Neil Cossons wrote that concrete,

> ... based on sand a gravel aggregate, is the defining construction material of the Cold War age. From it were created miles of runways and dispersal bays, observer posts and bunkers, hardened shelters, missile launch pads and test stands. And much else besides.[11]

Barnton Quarry

Barnton Quarry, near Edinburgh, was a three-level underground bunker and one of 14 Regional Seats of Government where key politicians and officials were expected to form a wartime Government in the event of a nuclear attack.

Courtesy of Barnton Bunker

In Scotland, as elsewhere on both sides of the Iron Curtain (which also used a significant amount of concrete), concrete was so widespread in both military and civilian construction that it 'could be thought of as a strategic weapon in the Cold War'.[12] And yet, in this book we have shown how pervasive the Cold War was in many other arenas of life beyond infrastructure. If we know where to look, there are many other materials, many other things, left to us.

Collecting the Cold War

Whether or not concrete is indeed characteristic of our experience of th Cold War today, one structure is clearly emblematic. The Berlin Wall was constructed in 1961 from barbed wire, then gradually replaced with fences and concrete sections over the next three decades. When it was torn down, those present felt the structure was sufficiently significant that they broke off sections of it and kept them. Some were sizeable, but some fitted in pockets or hand luggage, and there are now pieces of the wall all over the world – many more, suspiciously, than could ever have been part of the original.

Small chunks of the Wall thereby became keepsakes, souvenirs of the Cold War. There is no way of knowing how many authentic fragments came to Scotland, but a genuine piece came into the possession of Canon Kenyon Wright, the priest and politician who was so active in prompting peace across the Iron Curtain (see page 103), and it is now on display in the National Museum of Scotland. Indeed Canon Wright is far from the only 'keepsake keeper' who has contributed to museum collections and exhibitions.

The improvised rattle bottle of peace campaigner Kristin Barrett (see pages 76–77), tourist Eileen Crowford's *znachki* (see pages 98–99), survive not only because Barrett and Crowford consciously afforded meaning to them, but also because they were then passed to a public museum collection. Few can be seen on display at any one time, but they are meticulously imaged, catalogued and stored in the collections facility of National Museums Scotland, available for temporary display or for those interested in studying them.

The public memory of the Cold War, then, extends from missiles and bunkers to postcards, badges and improvised rattles; and those whose voices might otherwise have been lost to history can be accessed through their objects.[13] Material culture provides different perspectives on the Cold War.

The multi-disciplinary collections facility of National Museums Scotland houses not only Crowford's and Barrett's keepsakes, but also materials from around the world, further evidence of the connections to and from Scotland. There are textiles from the Soviet Bloc, for example, and artworks illustrating the Chinese Cultural Revolution, which was important to the global power balance (see page 91).

Piece of the Berlin Wall

After the dramatic events of 9/10 November 1989, the Berlin Wall was gradually dismantled. Many took the opportunity to save a memento of the Wall: this piece belonged to Canon Kenyon Wright, who had been active in building relationships with Warsaw Pact nations throughout the period.

Image © National Museums Scotland

Closer to home, as the ROC was disbanded, curators collected the complete contents of a monitoring post. As a window into the experience of monitoring and readiness, these artefacts are unparalleled (see Chapter 2).[14] The Corps has thereby left a very rich heritage, helping us to understand how civilian and military aspects of the Cold War overlapped.

The ROC volunteers' uniforms and the equipment of the post – ranging from devices to measure radioactivity, maps and tables, to more mundane items such as mugs and toilet paper – tell rich stories about how volunteers and governmental authorities imagined the reality of nuclear war.

In essence, the bunkers and their equipment were seen as miniature versions of a perfect society under attack: well-ordered and disciplined, well-informed through scientific knowledge, highly professional yet based on voluntary commitment, calm and rational when confronted with adversity. They emphasise the importance of maintaining social (law and) order in the face of catastrophe.

Radiation detectors (see pages 60–61) are perhaps archetypal Cold War artefacts and, not surprisingly, other radiation detectors in museum collections come from the nuclear industry. Nuclear heritage extends from the sites mentioned above to objects and records from them. The Nuclear Decommissioning Authority incudes heritage in its remit and passes a selection of artefacts to museums for posterity, enhancing the growing field of 'nuclear cultural heritage'.[15] This brings new objects into the public domain, often for the first time.

The largest and most striking artefacts in museums that remain to remind us of the global conflict are military. Perhaps most awesome of all are the weapons themselves. Polaris missiles are surprisingly common in British museums, including the National Museum of Flight at East Fortune, but artillery and hand weapons also survive. The paraphernalia of the military is collected by veterans and their families, by regiments and by public museums. As with other eras and conflicts, this includes medals and uniforms.

While the Imperial War Museum was not successful in its attempt to acquire a nuclear submarine in the 1970s, there are aircraft in museums across Britain, from V-bombers such as the Vulcan at East Fortune to the staggering Lockheed SR-71 Blackbird at the American Air Museum in Duxford, a reconnaissance aircraft once the fastest in the world.[16] Road vehicles survive in great numbers, from tanks to civil defence motorbikes, although fewer are retained in collections than from the Second World War.

Likewise, more museum exhibits are devoted to the First and Second World Wars than the Cold War, but there are opportunities to see this material culture on display. Among earlier material, if one looks for it, Cold War material can be found within the displays at the National War Museum in Edinburgh and the National Museum of Flight. In these and other military museums, there has been a shift from exhibiting guns, armour and weapons towards highlighting the fact that wars are about killing and dying. Such

Long Live Chairman Mao porcelain vase, Jingdezhen, 1968

Artworks from Chinese Cultural Revolution can be found in the National Museum of Scotland. *This Long Live Chairman Mao porcelain vase has Mao's poem The Double Ninth on reverse.*

Image © National Museums Scotland

Opposite, above: Polaris missile

This British Polaris submarine-launched ballistic missile is an Active Inert Missile (AIM) without an active warhead used for training purposes. This example is from the Imperial War Museum's Collection.

Kumar Sriskandan / Alamy Stock Photo

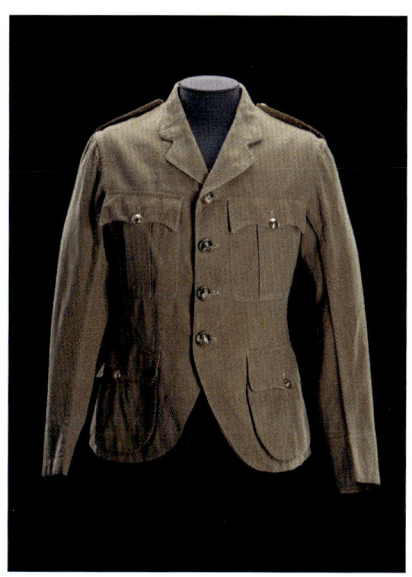

Cameron Highlander jacket

This uniform with Cameron Highlander regiment buttons and shoulder titles, was worn by Captain A. A. Fairrie in the late 1950s. The battalion was based in Aden Colony, now part of Yemen, and guarded the BP oil refinery.

Image © National Museums Scotland

Green Goddess fire engine

From the mid-1950s, a fleet of heavy-duty Bedford RLHZ self-propelled pump fire engines nicknamed 'Green Goddesses' were stationed at East Fortune. These fire engines would have been used by the Auxiliary Fire Service to back up the regular fire service in the event of a nuclear attack.

Image © National Museums Scotland

interpretations focus on the role of people in war and the military, an approach that suits the subtleties of the 'imaginary war' of the Cold War.

Rarer than military technology on display is the art and design of the Cold War. In 2014 the Victoria and Albert Museum in London staged the exhibition *Cold War Modern: Design 1945–1970*, exploring design ideas from furniture, motorcars, graphics and architecture; and there are significant holdings in National Museums Scotland and the V&A Dundee that are now framed in this context.[17] The Cold War thereby becomes a mid-century design motif, removed from conflict and toxic landscapes.

These museum displays are evidence of the relationship between the Cold War and designers at the time; over the decades, many artists have generated work reflecting on the legacies of the Cold War. Among them is the photographer and sculptor Michael Sanders, who explores the leftovers and active presence of nuclear weapons in the Scottish landscape.

In his 'nuclear tourist' persona, he photographs himself near sites including Coulport. In many of these, he wears clothing made from the Polaris

Military tartan (see page 26). Sanders has also designed and registered the 'SALT3 Submarine' tartan to highlight pollution around the Clydeside and other submarine bases in the United Kingdom; a sample is in the collection of National Museums Scotland.[18]

Spanning this disciplinary range, this book accompanies an exhibition, also *Cold War Scotland*, at the National Museum of Scotland in 2024. It intends to present material from across the lived experience, not only nuclear weapons but also mobilisations and connections.

As such the exhibition at National Museums Scotland has followed the multi-disciplinary approach of the *100 Objects: Berlin During the Cold War* exhibition held at the Alliierten (Allied) Museum in Berlin (2016).[19] That exhibition displayed material culture from a wide range of aspects of life, from board games to flags to traffic cones, juxtaposing high politics and espionage with humdrum existence in the city. The range of objects on display there afforded visitors a unique glimpse of Cold War everyday life in Berlin for its citizens – including, refreshingly, the material culture of the domestic realm, such as kitchen technology and children's toys. There is a great diversity of material culture that can help us to remember the Cold War. These artefacts had different meanings for different people at the time. For some, the military installations and weapons were primarily markers of security and shelter, for others, they signified the fear of destruction. For many, a nuclear submarine was a place of work; for others, it was a symbol of the destruction of society. Artefacts from power stations might be legacies of risk, or remnants of industry, innovation and economic change.

Whereas the CND regarded itself and its symbols and songs as the standard bearer of democracy, others saw it as a threat to Scottish society. Today many of these artefacts seem to have lost their polemical character; we might look at technological objects like the Polaris missile mostly in awe and we might smile at some of the jokes on the badges.

Left and above: Michael Sanders and the 'SALT3 Submarine' tartan

British sculptor and photographer Michael Sanders creates art as a 'blundering nuclear tourist' to highlight the legacy of Cold War and nuclear sites around the UK. Michael is wearing a Polaris Military tartan suit across the bay from Coulport, north Holy Loch. Sanders produced the 'SALT3 Submarine' tartan in response to the pollution around Britain caused by submarine bases. The rust red represents the rust of decommissioned submarines, with the blue, green and greys referring to the pollutants Cobalt-60, Tritium and Carbon-14. The grey also refers to the suits worn by decision-makers in Westminster.
Michael Sanders

Opposite: Civil Defence Corps motorcycle

The Civil Defence Corps was part of a chain of emergency organisations, including the fire and ambulance brigades, who would respond to a nuclear attack. Communications between emergency responders would have been crucial in the aftermath of an attack so vehicles like this motorcycle were vital.

Image © National Museums Scotland

It is the role of museums and other heritage organisations to offer different interpretations of artworks and artefacts in their displays. Cold War exhibitions may celebrate the success of the West, or else emphasise commonalities across the Iron Curtain; they may present Cold War heritage as celebratory or difficult.[20] But whatever the intention of curators, displays impact visitors in different ways, depending on what the visitor brings with them: their experiences, their perspectives, their memories.

Historical study can connect these Cold War materials to their place, but it might be an interesting experiment to imagine some of the objects illustrated in this chapter in places out in the real world today. How do the objects change their meaning if we imagine them in a different setting? And how does this change our view of the objects as well as the part of Cold War history that they represent?

To those who remember the Cold War, the objects discussed here may invoke fear or nostalgia, national pride or shame. A military installation might provoke anxiety, or bring back feelings of security. A protest banner might represent a standard of democracy, or a threat to Scottish society. A missile might be awful or awesome.

'Shoemakers say cobblers to the bomb' badge

A badge from the Kristin Barrett anti-nuclear collection highlighting the light-hearted nature of some elements of the CND campaign.

Image © National Museums Scotland

Notes

1. Samuel J. M. M. Alberti, 'The Vulcan's Voice: multiple meanings of a Cold War artefact', in Jessica Douthwaite et al. (eds), *Cold War Museology* (London: Routledge, 2024).
2. Matthew Grant and Benjamin Ziemann (eds), *Understanding the Imaginary War: Culture, Thought and Nuclear Conflict* (Manchester: Manchester University Press, 2016); John Schofield and Wayne Cocroft (eds), *A Fearsome Heritage: Diverse Legacies of the Cold War* (Walnut Creek, CA: Left Coast, 2007).
3. Brian P. Jamison, (ed.), *Scotland and the Cold War* (Dunfermline: Cualann Press, 2009), p. 29.
4. Alex Boyd, 'Scottish Military Pastoral', *Studies in Photography* (Summer 2023), pp. 11–29, p. 24. https://studiesinphotography.com/.
5. Ian Brown, *Radar in Scotland 1938–46* (Edinburgh: Society of Antiquaries of Scotland, 2022).
6. Trevor Royle, *Facing the Bear: Scotland and the Cold War* (Edinburgh: Birlinn, 2019).
7. http://portal.historicenvironment.scot/designation/LB52578.
8. Paul Ozorak, *Underground Structures of the Cold War: The World Below* (Barnsley: Pen & Sword, 2012).
9. Linda M. Ross, 'Nuclear Cultural Heritage: From Energy Past to Heritage Future', *Heritage & Society* (2023), pp. 1–20.
10. https://www.gov.scot/policies/nuclear-energy/nuclear-stations/.
11. Neil Cossons, 'Foreword', in Wayne D. Cocroft, Roger J. C. Thomas and P. S. Barnwell (ed.), *Cold War: Building for Nuclear Confrontation, 1946–1989* (Swindon: Historic England, 2004), p. vii.
12. Adrian Forty, *Concrete and Culture: A Material History* (London: Reaktion Books, 2013), p. 160.
13. Sarah A. Harper, 'Bombers, Bunkers, and Badges. The Cold War Materialised in National Museums Scotland', unpublished PhD thesis, University of Stirling, 2022.
14. Sarah A. Harper, 'Readiness for Red Alert: Engaging with the Royal Observer Corps Material Culture', in Jessica Douthwaite et al. (eds), *Cold War Museology* (London: Routledge, 2024).
15. Ross, 'Nuclear Cultural Heritage'.
16. Paul Cornish, 'Extremes of collecting at the Imperial War Museum 1917–2009: Struggles with the large and the ephemeral', in Graeme Were and J. C. H. King (eds), *Extreme Collecting: Challenging Practices for 21st Century Museums* (New York, 2012), pp. 157–67.
17. David Crowley and Jane Pavitt (eds.), *Cold War Modern: Design 1945–1970* (London: V&A, 2008).
18. www.tartanregister.gov.uk/tartanDetails?ref=13810.
19. Berndt Von Kostka and Arno Helwig (eds) *100 Objects: Berlin during the Cold War* (Berlin: Berlin Story Verlag, 2016).
20. Samuel J. M. M. Alberti and Holger Nehring, 'The Cold War in European museums – filling the 'empty battlefield', *International Journal of Heritage Studies* 28 (2022), pp. 180–99.

Opposite: Black Knight rocket

The Black Knight was a liquid propellant research rocket produced by the Royal Aircraft Establishment and manufacturer Sanders-Roe Ltd in the 1950s. The findings from tests of the Black Knight help inform the development of intermediate-range ballistic missiles such as Blue Streak.

Image © National Museums Scotland

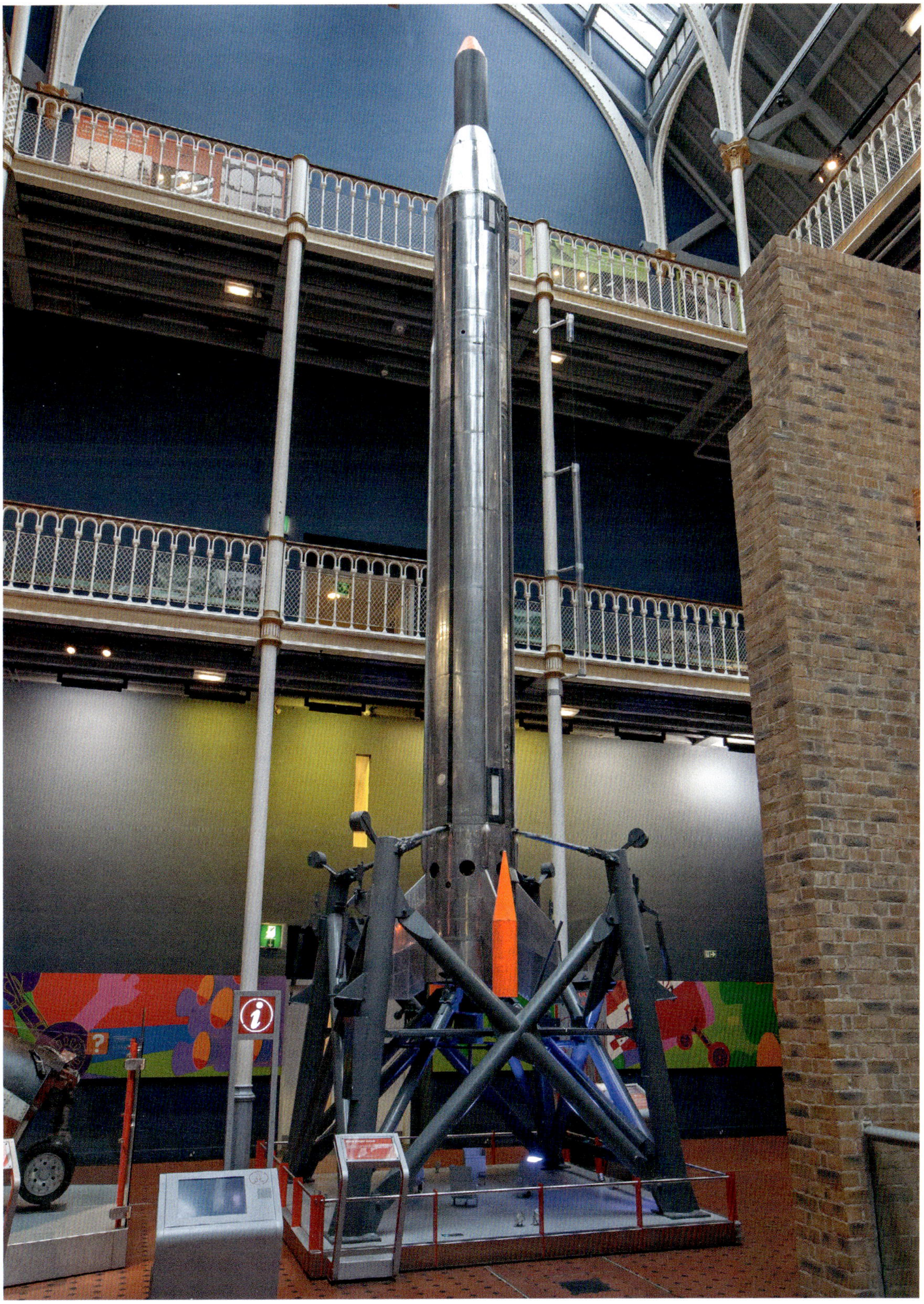

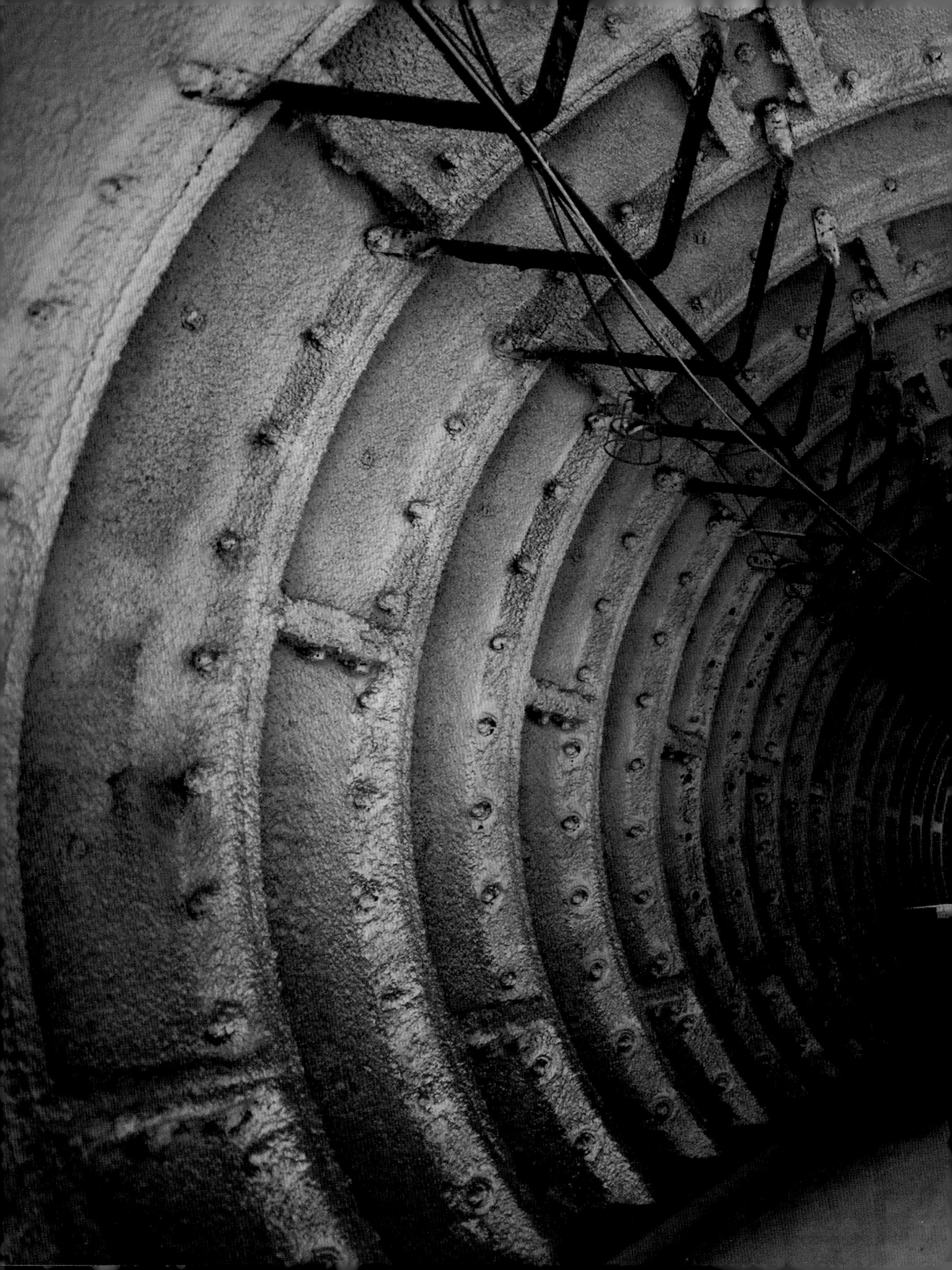

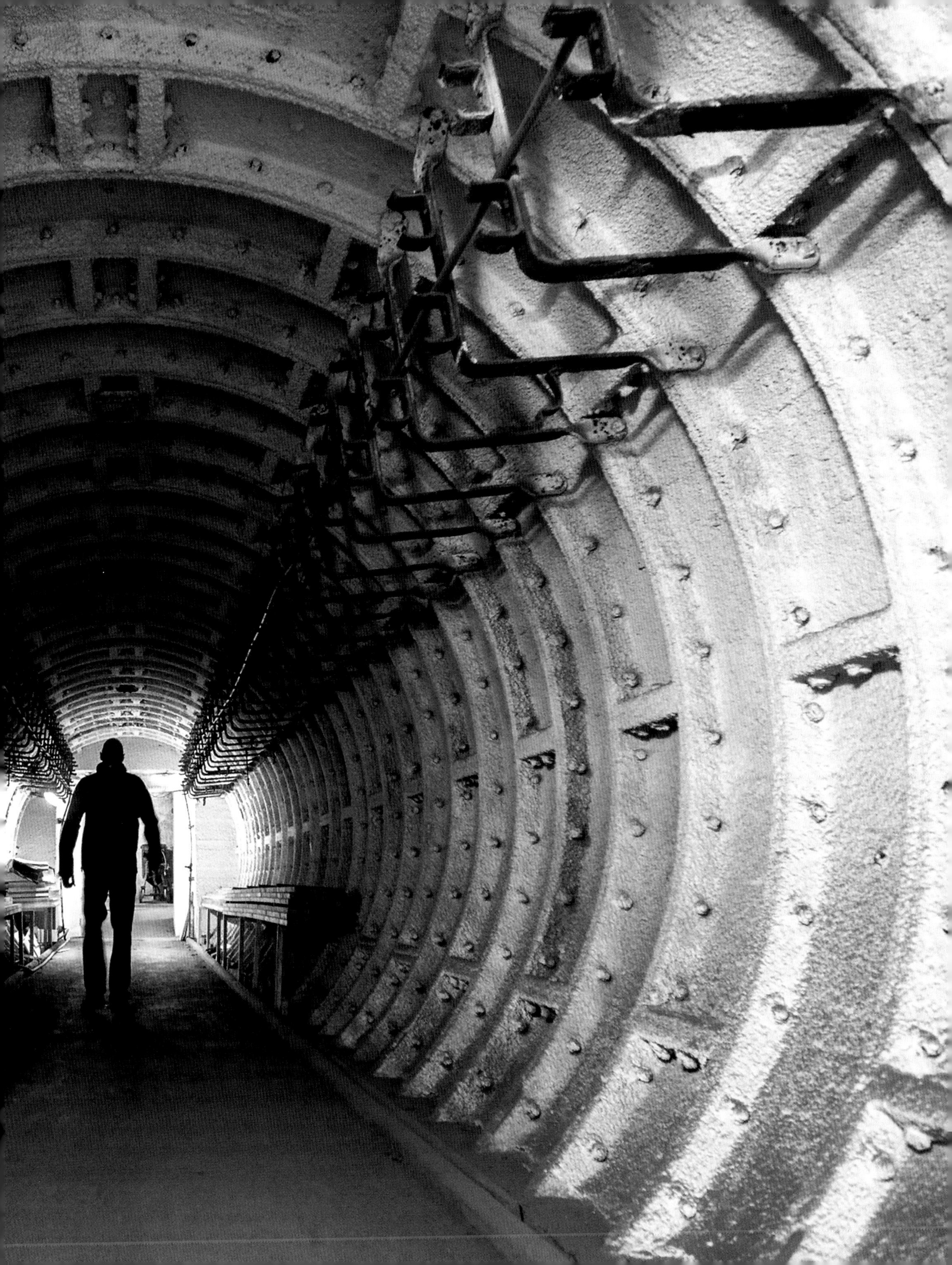

Epilogue

Sensing the Cold War

Cold War Scotland has focused on the material memories of the Cold War. Much of the experience of the Cold War, however, is immaterial. As discussed in Chapter 3, the culture of the Cold War endures in its literature, music and poetry. If a wider exploration of the intangible heritage of the Cold War in Scotland is the subject for another book, the material remains explored here are manifestations of the immaterial: whether of fear of attack, fear of radiation, fear of the unknown and unseen; or else hopes for a brighter future, of international collaboration.

Throughout the book, we have highlighted the kaleidoscopic nature of the Cold War in Scotland: of different experiences and emotions that involved both hopes and fears, often at the same time. And although Scotland was often the object of decision-making in London and Washington as well as in NATO, Scots never lost their agency – they were not just mobilised in and for the Cold War, they also played an active role in mobilising themselves or in resisting mobilisation.

Scotland therefore offers an excellent case study for challenging some of our assumptions of the Cold War in Britain more generally, by emphasising the importance of the north – and the North Atlantic – and by allowing us to examine the impact of the Cold War especially clearly.

There is, however, another aspect of the Cold War kaleidoscope that emerges when we look at objects and material culture. Kaleidoscopes are toys, little tubes that contain mirrors and pieces of coloured glass or plastic. When the tube is turned, different patterns emerge for the viewer. So let us look at the different colours and images that Cold War mobilisations in Scotland might create. While we might see the arms race in a threatening red – or as an icy white with a burning fire visible underneath – the Cold War as it played out in Scottish society evokes a different set of colours. It was as grey as the concrete of the many military installations that were built as part of Cold War mobilisations and that were dug deep into the Scottish landscape, or as silver and metallic as the steel and aluminium produced by the defence industry in Scotland.

Pages 122–23: Barnton Quarry tunnel

The former ROTOR station and later Regional Seat of Government at Barnton Quarry, Edinburgh, transferred ownership to Lothian Regional Council in 1983. In 2021, Historic Environment Scotland designated the site as Category A listed. It is currently being renovated with plans to open as a visitor attraction.

SWNS Media Group

Opposite: Polaris missile

A Royal Navy Polaris A3 missile fired from the nuclear-powered submarine HMS *Resolution*, off Cape Kennedy (now Cape Canaveral).

© Imperial War Museum (MH 30564)

But it could also be more colourful, like some of the banners of the CND, or the pink toilet paper from an ROC post that can be found in the collections of National Museums Scotland. Only rarely did it come in the khaki colour of the Civil Defence Corps motorcycle (see page 119) – the military side of the Cold War managed to hide quite well, it seems. Like the Polaris Military tartan the Cold War in Scotland was neither monochrome nor immutable. Rather it was a complex, mutable weave, comprising many individual threads.

Cold War mobilisations also had sounds; not the sounds of marching boots, but the sounds of air raid sirens used during tests. Or the sounds blaring out of a grey speaker that was part of an installation found in chaplaincies, pubs or post offices across Scotland. Such speakers were named Handel, after the baroque Anglo-German composer George Frederick Handel, alluding to the hymn 'Sound an Alarm' in his oratorio *Judas Maccabaeus*. Their purpose was to transmit a warning of an impending nuclear attack or a warning of nuclear fallout if all other communications systems failed.

The sounds of the Cold War were also the sounds of the machinery in the shipbuilding and ordnance factories in Scotland's Central Belt, or the sound of folk music on CND marches.

But often the sound of the Cold War was simply silence: the silence of concentration in an electronics lab; the silence of waiting for an attack, the silence after a supersonic boom, the silence of hope.

Thinking about these material and audio memories is to evoke the aura of the surviving objects. The aura of fighter bombers and rockets as both technological wonders and awesome death machines; the aura of declassified papers and formerly secret sites in letting the audience in on the often uncanny secrets of the Cold War state; the aura of empty uniforms; or the aura of empty and now disused airfields and bunkers enabling visitors to imagine what the Cold War was like. These are hooks for the stories told in this book.

Keeping these objects, and recording the memories they provoke, are all the more important as we gradually lose the generations who remember. The Scottish experience of the Cold War had a great deal in common with the rest of the United Kingdom, the West, and even the Soviet Union. Nevertheless, with its distinct topography, position and culture, Scotland's experience of the Cold War has been a colourful story to tell.

Handel warning system speaker

A broadcast system loudspeaker that was part of the Handel system. Supposed to give the public a warning of imminent attack, the communications system was nicknamed 'Handel' after the composer of the aria, 'Sound an Alarm'.

Image © National Museums Scotland

Further reading

Bartie, Angela, *The Edinburgh Festivals: Culture and Society in Post-war Britain* (Edinburgh: Edinburgh University Press, 2013).

Bud, Robert and Philip Gummett (eds), *Cold War, Hot Science: Applied Research in Britain's Defence Laboratories, 1945–1990* (Amsterdam: Harwood Academic/Science Museum, 1999).

Chamberlin, Paul, *The Cold War's Killing Fields* (New York: Harper, 2018).

Cocroft, Wayne D., Roger J. C. Thomas and P. S. Barnwell (eds), *Cold War: Building for Nuclear Confrontation, 1946–1989* (Swindon: Historic England, 2004).

Crowley, David and Jane Pavitt (eds), *Cold War Modern: Design 1945–1970* (London: V&A, 2008).

Davies, John and Alexander J. Kent, *The Red Atlas: How the Soviet Union Secretly Mapped the World* (Chicago: University of Chicago Press, 2017).

Douthwaite, Jessica, Samuel J. M. M. Alberti and Holger Nehring (eds), *Cold War Museology* (London: Routledge, 2024).

Edgerton, David, *Warfare State: Britain, 1920–1970* (Cambridge: Cambridge University Press, 2006).

French, David, *Military Identities. The Regimental System, the British Army, & the British People, c.1870–2000* (Oxford University Press, 2005).

Grant, Matthew and Benjamin Ziemann (eds), *Understanding the Imaginary War: Culture, Thought and Nuclear Conflict* (Manchester: Manchester University Press, 2016).

Harper, Sarah A., *Chapelcross and the Cold War: Scotland's First Nuclear Power Station* (Eastriggs: Devil's Porridge Museum, 2018).

Harper, Sarah A., 'Bombers, Bunkers, and Badges. The Cold War Materialised in National Museums Scotland', unpublished PhD thesis, University of Stirling, 2022.

Hennessy, Peter and James Jinks, *The Silent Deep: The Royal Navy Submarine Service since 1945* (London: Allen Lane, 2015).

Hogg, Jonathan, *British Nuclear Culture: Official and Unofficial Narratives in the Long 20th Century* (London: Bloomsbury, 2016).

Jamieson, Brian P. (ed.), *Scotland and the Cold War* (Dunfermline: Cualann Press, 2003).

Knox, William W., *Industrial Nation: Work, Culture and Society in Scotland, 1800–Present* (Edinburgh: Edinburgh University Press, 1999).

Lavery, Brian, *Shield of Empire: The Royal Navy and Scotland* (Edinburgh: Birlinn, 2007).

MacKenzie, John and Tom M. Devine (eds), *Scotland and the British Empire* (Oxford: Oxford University Press, 2011).

Ozorak, Paul, *Underground Structures of the Cold War: The World Below* (Barnsley: Pen & Sword, 2012).

Petrie, Malcolm, *Politics and the People: Scotland, 1945–1979* (Edinburgh: Edinburgh University Press, 2022).

Ross, Linda M., Katrina Navickas, Matthew Kelly, and Ben Anderson (eds), *New Lives, New Landscapes Revisited: Rural Modernity in Britain* (Oxford: Oxford University Press, 2023).

Royle, Trevor, *Facing the Bear: Scotland and the Cold War* (Edinburgh: Birlinn, 2019).

Schofield, John and Wayne D. Cocroft (eds), *A Fearsome Heritage: Diverse Legacies of the Cold War* (Walnut Creek, CA: Left Coast, 2007).

Spaven, Malcolm, *Fortress Scotland: A Guide to the Military Presence* (London: Pluto Press, 1983).

Spiers, Edward M., Jeremy A. Crang and Matthew J. Strickland (eds), *A Military History of Scotland* (Edinburgh: Edinburgh University Press, 2012).

Vinen, Richard, *National Service. Conscription in Britain 1945–1963* (London: Allen Lane, 2014).

Westad, Odd Arne, *Global Cold War: Third World Interventions and the Making of our Times* (Cambridge: Cambridge University Press, 2007).

Young, Taras, *Nuclear War in the UK* (London: Four Corners, 2019).

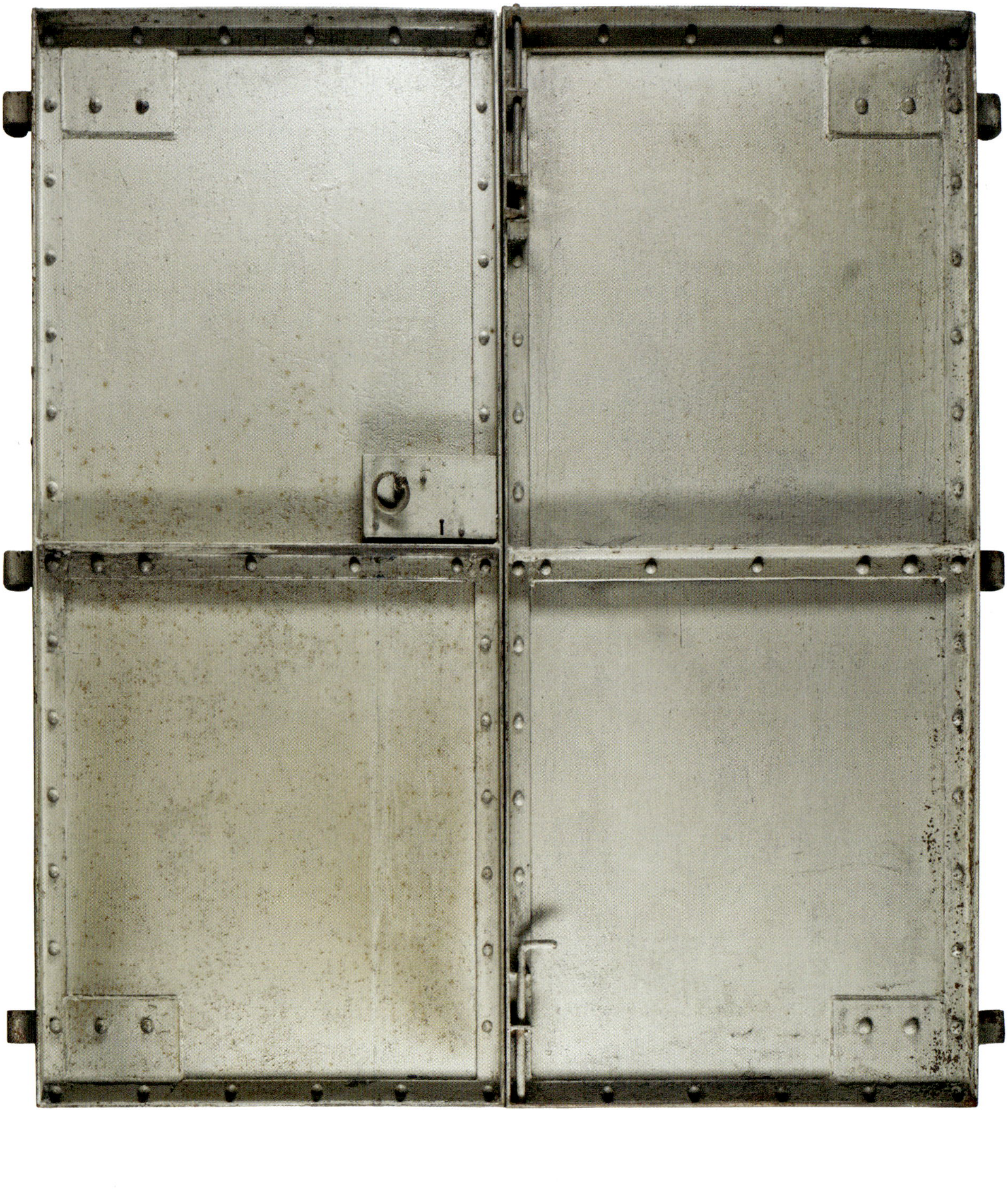